E-WASTE

By David M. Barker

ECOLOGICAL **DISASTERS**

Content Consultant

Peter Little
Assistant Professor of Anthropology
Rhode Island College

Essential Library
An Imprint of Abdo Publishing | abdopublishing.com

abdopublishing.com

Published by Abdo Publishing, a division of ABDO, PO Box 398166, Minneapolis, Minnesota 55439. Copyright © 2018 by Abdo Consulting Group, Inc. International copyrights reserved in all countries. No part of this book may be reproduced in any form without written permission from the publisher. Essential Library™ is a trademark and logo of Abdo Publishing.

Printed in the United States of America, North Mankato, Minnesota
042017
092017

THIS BOOK CONTAINS
RECYCLED MATERIALS

Cover Photo: Johannes Eisele/AFP/Getty Images
Interior Photos: Norman NG/KRT/Newscom, 4; Marie Bobrovskaya/Shutterstock Images, 6; Natalie Behring/TCS/ZumaPress/Newscom, 8, 54, 61, 99; Chen jie gx/Imaginechina/AP Images, 10, 98 (middle); iStockphoto, 12–13, 17, 18, 22, 24, 27, 30–31, 35, 45, 47, 51, 56, 63, 79, 83, 84–85, 92–93; Peter Stackpole/The LIFE Picture Collection/Getty Images, 15, 98 (left); Paul Sakuma/AP Images, 19; Red Line Editorial, 20, 33, 34, 77, 95; Zoran Milich/Moment Mobile/Getty Images, 28, 98 (right); SPL/Science Source, 36, 41; Ouedraogo Nyaba/SIPA/Newscom, 38, 55; Charles D. Winters/Science Source, 43; Tyrone Siu/Reuters/Newscom, 48–49; Dibyangshu Sarkar/AFP/Getty Images, 53; James MacDonald/Bloomberg/Getty Images, 58; Michael Reynolds/EPA/Newscom, 64–65, 70–71; Rene van Bakel/ASAblanca/Getty Images, 67; Jie Zhao/Corbis News/Getty Images, 75; Jagadeesh Nv/EPA/Newscom, 76; Michael Conroy/AP Images, 86–87; Dirk Wiersma/Science Source, 91; Shutterstock Images, 97

Editor: Marie Pearson
Series Designer: Laura Polzin

Publisher's Cataloging-in-Publication Data

Names: Barker, David M., author.
Title: E-waste / by David M. Barker.
Description: Minneapolis, MN : Abdo Publishing, 2018. | Series: Ecological disasters | Includes bibliographical references and index.
Identifiers: LCCN 2016962232 | ISBN 9781532110221 (lib. bdg.) | ISBN 9781680788075 (ebook)
Subjects: LCSH: Electronic waste--Juvenile literature. | Electronic apparatus and appliances--Juvenile literature. | Refuse and refuse disposal--Juvenile literature. | Environmental degradation--Juvenile literature. | Ecological disturbances--Juvenile literature.
Classification: DDC 363.738--dc23
LC record available at http://lccn.loc.gov/2016962232

CONTENTS

Most of the e-waste recycled at Guiyu came from outside of China.

Chapter
ONE

A HEALTH AND ENVIRONMENTAL DISASTER

Guiyu is a collection of 28 villages in Guangdong Province in southern China. It has approximately 132,000 inhabitants and 100,000 migrant workers.[1] From the 1990s until 2015, 60 to 80 percent of the families in Guiyu made a living recycling electronic waste, or e-waste.[2] They worked out of almost 6,000 family businesses.[3] These were informal businesses, and the workplaces were unregulated. The town was notorious for unhealthy work conditions.

ELECTRONICS

In the middle of the 1900s, many home electronics such as radios and televisions used vacuum tubes to control electrical currents in ways that made the product work. These large glass-and-metal tubes connected to other parts of the electronic circuit on a circuit board that held everything in place. Because they are smaller and use less energy, transistors eventually replaced vacuum tubes. Then integrated circuits (ICs), or chips, replaced large numbers of transistors and other components. ICs are called chips because they are made on a chip or flake of silicon. Some ICs contain millions of components within a small area.[4] ICs attach to a circuit board, which connects to other electronic components. Metals that conduct electricity connect all of the components on a circuit board. The board itself is made of glass fibers and epoxy (a tough polymer, or glue) mixed with a flame retardant.

Chinese scientists documented methods used to separate the materials in the e-waste. Workers baked circuit boards over coal fires to remove electronic components. Workers soaked circuit boards in acid baths to extract precious metals such as gold and palladium. They dumped the acid waste onto nearby fields or in streams. Sometimes they stripped plastic from wires and cables or burned the plastic in open air to release the copper wire inside. Workers burned fragments of plastics to identify the type of plastic by smell. To remove valuable metals, they hammered open many components, including batteries, transformers, and computer monitors containing heavy glass cathode-ray tubes (CRTs). For the most part, workers carried out their tasks without protective equipment. Children either helped process the materials or played with discarded electronic components.

These processes exposed the workers and their children to dangerous levels of toxic chemicals. The toxins increased miscarriages and premature births. Toxins were also related to children's lung health, growth rates, and behavior. The processes polluted the air, dust, and drinking water with poisonous levels of heavy metals. Many films and photographs documented the conditions in Guiyu. These images dramatically showed the human health risks, poor working environment, and environmental damage in and around Guiyu.

TOXIC DUMPING?

For more than a decade, Guiyu and similar places in other developing nations have represented the ugly side of Western countries' throwaway culture, especially that of the United States. In throwaway cultures, consumers buy cheap electronics, use them for a year or two, and then discard them without worrying about where the waste ends up.

Guiyu has been the subject of many news articles, photographic essays, a 2001 film documentary, and a 2008 news documentary. These stories contain powerful images of piles of discarded electronics and cluttered workshops where workers roast circuit boards over open fires. Images from Africa show young men standing in muddy fields surrounded by electronic debris and tending flaming balls of plastic-coated copper wires, the wires puffing poisonous black smoke. Many of these stories say that the United States and other developed countries are dumping unwanted e-waste into developing nations. In developing nations, workers who informally recycle e-waste are

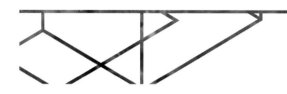

FORMAL VERSUS INFORMAL RECYCLING

Recycling can be part of a regulated or unregulated economy. A garage sale is an example of an unregulated, or informal, business activity. It operates alongside formal businesses, such as bookstores, pawn shops, and antique stores, that buy and sell used items. The stores pay taxes, have accountants who manage their money, and may be required to follow certain governmental regulations. Garage sales account for a lot of money changing hands, but they are a part of the informal economy. They do not pay taxes or follow regulations like formal businesses do. Informal recyclers, such as those in Guiyu, operate as informal businesses.

A worker in Guiyu uses a lighter to burn plastic off a copper wire. Burning plastic releases toxic chemicals.

unprotected by regulations. Poor workers without any other way to earn a living are recycling the waste in dangerous conditions. The informal recycling trade damages the workers' health and the environment.

Guiyu and other places where e-waste is recycled informally have earned a horrific reputation from news stories and documentaries. But the stories are also misleading in some ways. Exported electronics are not all waste to be dumped on developing countries that do not want them. Shipments of electronics have been tracked to Ghana in Africa. The electronics were mostly reused by people there. These reused electronics bridge the so-called digital divide. The digital divide is the large difference in people's abilities to get computers and Internet access in developing and developed nations.

The problem is also not that developing countries are recycling e-waste. The materials that are recycled have value, or the recyclers would not take the time to extract them. It is also important that the materials in e-waste be recycled to avoid having to mine new materials, which requires energy and causes environmental damage. Recycling e-waste may be the only way some workers can earn a living. The problem is with how e-waste is recycled, and the question is how to ensure the safety of workers and the environment.

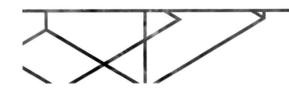

WASTE VERSUS SCRAP

Although the term e-waste is commonly used, it is not completely accurate. E-waste is actually one form of what is known as scrap, or discarded materials that are suitable for recycling. Some of the most valuable forms of scrap are metals. There is a worldwide trade in scrap that is an important part of the economy. Trading and processing scrap provides work opportunities for many people. Trading and recycling scrap metal helps avoid mining new metal. It takes much less energy to make new products out of recycled metals than newly mined metals. Scrap trade makes economies more efficient and conserves limited resources.

A MOUNTAIN OF E-WASTE

The world produced 46.1 million short tons (41.8 million metric tons) of e-waste in 2014. This is about the weight of 200,000 large passenger jets, enough jets to line up between New York, New York, and Los Angeles, California, four times. This waste is made up of mostly large and small appliances such as microwaves and dishwashers, but it also includes

E-waste produced in 2014 included 3.3 million short tons (3 million metric tons) of computers, cell phones, and other information technology equipment.

devices such as computers. The total amount has been growing each year. Asia produces most of that waste, followed by the Americas and Europe. But on a per-person basis, both Europe and the Americas lead in producing e-waste. Their citizens produce four to five times as much e-waste per person as people living in Asia.[5]

E-waste production will continue to increase. Extracting its materials for reuse and providing jobs for workers will become more and more important. The countries that are best suited to recycle e-waste are those that need the raw materials most. Those countries are developing countries such as China and India, which are manufacturing the world's electronic products and building their own cities. Those products, buildings, highways, and electric systems need the steel, copper, and aluminum in e-waste. However, the technology of recycling e-waste and building greener products must be developed to make recycling safer. The responsibility for this rests on both developed and developing nations. Many existing laws are meant to force countries that produce e-waste to find ways to safely recycle it. In the coming years, nations will have to cooperate to solve this growing problem.

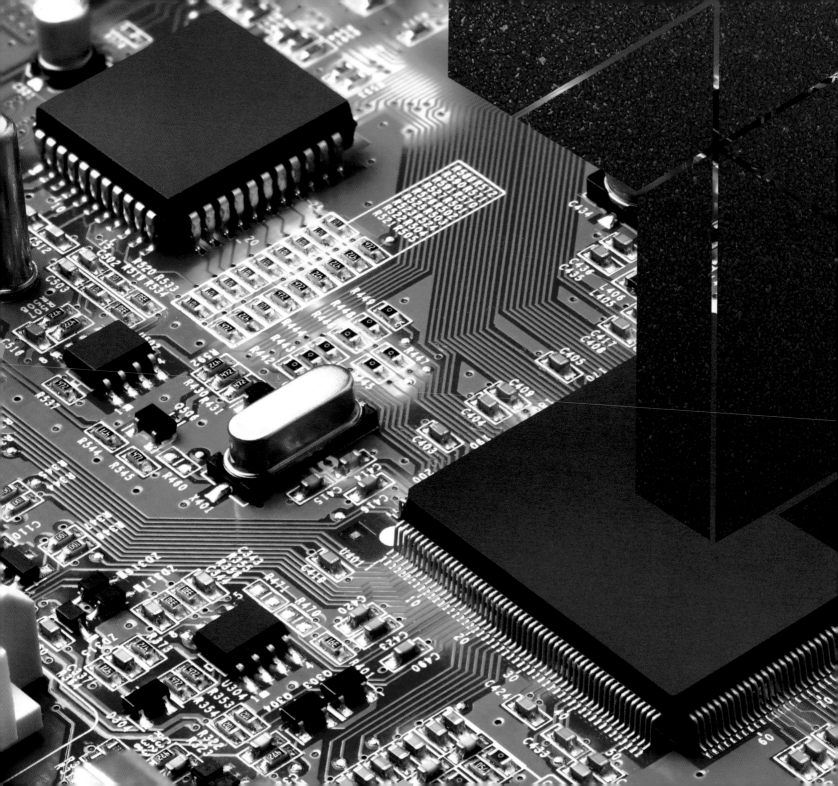

TWO

WHAT IS E-WASTE?

E-waste is defined in different ways. The strictest definition of e-waste includes only devices with electronic circuits. Electronic circuits have parts in them that control the flow of electricity, such as transistors or integrated circuits (which are commonly called chips). The electronic parts contain dangerous materials, but also valuable ones such as gold and silver.

Another category that can be included under e-waste is electric devices. Electric devices, such as refrigerators or stoves, use energy to make things like heat or motion. They

Chips are used in devices such as computers, cell phones, game consoles, televisions, and modems.

did not include electronic controls. However, more of these electric appliances now have electronic controls, so they are considered e-waste even though they may be mostly made of steel and plastic. When researchers, the European Union, or the United Nations measure e-waste, typically both electronic and electric devices are included in a category called waste electric and electronic equipment, or WEEE. The description of what e-waste actually includes and how it is measured is important for understanding where e-waste is being produced, transported, and recycled or dumped.

THROWAWAY SOCIETY

E-waste is a growing problem. The amount of waste, including e-waste, the United States produces is increasing. It is increasing because the population is growing and because each American produces more waste each year. In the United States between 1960 and 2013, the total amount of trash rose from 88.1 million short tons (79.9 million metric tons) to 254.1 million short tons (230.5 million metric tons) per year. The amount of trash one person made increased from 2.68 pounds (1.22 kg) per day in 1960 to 4.4 pounds (2 kg) per day in 2013.[1] These numbers suggest that more and more Americans live in what is called a throwaway society.

> "Municipal waste in industrialized countries has been increasing at around the same rate as economic growth, around 40 percent over the past 30 years."[2]
> —*Tim Cooper, Centre for Sustainable Consumption, Nottingham Trent University*

The 1955 *Life* magazine article "Throwaway Living" appears to have first used this term. The article's headline reads, "Disposable items cut down household chores." The article

Aluminum foil, paper plates, and straws were among the popular disposable items featured in the *Life* photo.

says, "The objects flying through the air in this picture would take 40 hours to clean—except that no housewife need bother. They are all meant to be thrown away after use."[3] This is an attractive message if throwing things away has no cost. It may have seemed that way in 1955. Today, the costs are better known. A throwaway society is based on consuming things and throwing them out when no longer useful. Some things are meant to be disposable. But even things that are used over and over, such as televisions, are thrown out more and more often.

Three features mark the United States' throwaway culture. First, it is a society based on consumption. The US economy depends on consumer demand for physical items such as refrigerators, microwaves, televisions, and cell phones. In a different kind of economy, consumers might desire music concerts, meetings with friends, or walks in the park. In the United States, making and selling tangible goods creates jobs. Those jobs provide the money needed to buy more products. This is an economy based on consumption. Some products save time and make life safer and easier than it was 100 years ago. Washing machines save time and a great deal of work. Refrigerators keep food from spoiling. Other items are considered luxuries, such as e-book readers, televisions, and tablets.

A second feature of the US throwaway society is the short life-span of many products. One measure of life-span might be the time until the first buyer of a device resells it, disposes of it, or otherwise stops using it. Or the life-span might be the time until a device breaks and cannot be repaired. Sometimes things can be fixed, but many products made today cannot be easily or cheaply fixed. If people do not fix a device, they often discard

In 2014, more than 1.8 million people in the United States were employed as assemblers and fabricators, building products including computers and electronic devices.

it. Measuring a product's life-span is a part of predicting how much e-waste will need to be recycled.

Few researchers have studied changes in products' life-spans. But the few studies on product life-spans indicate life-spans may be getting shorter. If this is true, it will add to the amount of e-waste over time. Researchers studied the life-spans of computers at a US

PLANNED OBSOLESCENCE

Planned obsolescence means designing a product so that it will wear out or become less wanted over time. General Motors may have started this trend. The company designed new models of cars each year so customers would want to replace their older models. The problem for product makers is that when everyone has something, the only way to increase sales is to make that thing with a shorter life-span. This strategy works best when there are few companies making a particular product. In electronics, especially computers, improvements such as speed, convenience, and capacity also contribute to obsolescence.

university between 1985 and 2000. They found the average life-span declined from about 10.7 years in 1985 to 5.5 years in 2000.[4] That's a one-half decrease in life-span in just 15 years. A study in Germany between 2004 and 2013 found similar results with household appliances. The number of appliances that needed to be replaced because they broke doubled during the study.[5]

The final feature of the United States' throwaway society is the unending parade of new and supposedly better products available to consumers. This parade encourages consumers to upgrade from a product that still works to a new product. The old product may find a second life with a new user who is happy with a less expensive, older model. However, these upgrades contribute to the number of new products made, sold, and eventually discarded.

Some new products are improvements to existing ones. But many new products, especially in electronics, are designed to help companies stay competitive. This is good for the company, but it has costs for consumers and for the environment. In a society that always wants the latest gadget, older models end up in landfills as consumers upgrade their devices. There are few incentives for companies to make products that will last longer or be easier to repair or recycle.

Companies regularly make improvements to devices to make consumers want to upgrade. They may build sharper screens or make devices thinner and lighter.

Computers have been an exception. Until recently, new computer models were in fact much better than the models produced just two or five years previously because of a steady and rapid growth in the computing power. This growth is described by Moore's Law, coined by Intel cofounder Gordon Moore. Moore observed that the number of components in an integrated circuit was doubling every year or two, making computers more powerful.[6]

HOW MUCH E-WASTE IS PRODUCED?

The amount of e-waste that the world produces is growing, and the trend shows no sign of stopping. Between 2010 and 2014, the United Nations estimated that the amount of

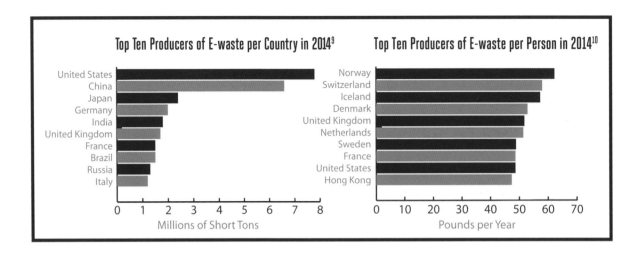

Top Ten Producers of E-waste per Country in 2014[9]

Top Ten Producers of E-waste per Person in 2014[10]

e-waste produced in the world each year increased from 37.3 million short tons (33.8 million metric tons) to 46.1 million short tons (41.8 million metric tons). This includes 3.3 million short tons (3 million metric tons) of computers, cell phones, and other information technology equipment. This number could climb to 54.9 million short tons (49.8 million metric tons) by 2018.[7]

The increase is not only due to global population growth. The amount of e-waste per person has been growing from 11 pounds (5 kg) per year in 2010 to a projected 14.8 pounds (6.7 kg) per year in 2018. The per-person rates are increasing even as the population is growing. The biggest waste producers are countries with some of the largest and wealthiest populations. The largest producer in 2014 was the United States, followed closely by China.[8]

The amounts per person form a very different list. The highest per-person amounts are mainly from European countries. The United States and China are lower on this list.

But there are many other wealthy countries that produce a lot of e-waste per person, even though their populations may be small.

Many of these countries ship e-waste to developing countries to be recycled. The United States, Canada, South Korea, Japan, Australia, and some European countries all export large quantities of e-waste illegally or disguised as equipment for reuse. Smaller amounts, such as 15 percent of e-waste in the United States, are disposed of legally within the countries they are collected in.[11] E-waste shipped to be recycled goes to China, India, several west African countries, Egypt, Brazil, Mexico, eastern Europe, and Southeast Asia. China also exports e-waste to Southeast Asian countries. In most of these places, the recycling is informal and unsafe.

Increasing restrictions on e-waste disposal in developed countries and the high costs of recycling in those countries drive the export of e-waste. A report by the International Labour Office, *The Global Impact of E-waste: Addressing the Challenge*, summarized the findings of a study that the US Environmental Protection Agency (EPA) commissioned. It says that "it was ten times cheaper to export e-waste to Asia than it was to process it in the United States. The incentives for e-waste movement, both legally and illegally, are thus enormous."[12] But the reduced production costs come at a price to those who work for unregulated businesses.

Recycling copper can use up to 85 percent less energy than producing copper from ores.[13]

Hazardous materials disposed of in landfills can harm the local wildlife.

Chapter
THREE

HOW E-WASTE IS MANAGED TODAY

E-waste contains a variety of resources. Some are valuable, and some are hazardous to health and the environment. The valuable and hazardous parts influence how e-waste is disposed of in developed countries. Some traditional methods of disposal, such as landfills and incinerators, are potentially dangerous destinations for e-waste.

Landfills, or dumps, are the main locations where cities dispose of their waste. A landfill is an area of land where waste is dumped and left to decompose. In many developed countries, landfill sites have a bottom layer that keeps liquids from

Landfills need to collect and treat leachate so it does not contaminate groundwater, which more than one-half of Americans rely on for drinking water.

seeping into groundwater. This protects groundwater from contaminants. Instead, pipes drain off the contaminated liquid. This liquid, called leachate, must be treated before it is released into the environment. Each day, the waste is covered with a layer of dirt to prevent unpleasant smells from leaving the landfill site. In many undeveloped countries, the waste is left uncovered except when it is covered by further layers of waste. Some landfills have no system to contain waste liquid that drains from the bottom of the landfill.

In the past, landfills were considered a solution for waste, where waste would never concern anyone ever again. But humanity's ever-increasing need for land has shown that no place is far enough away. Someone will need or want to live there one day or need to obtain water or grow things there. Ideally, the materials put into a landfill will eventually break down into their basic substances. This goal makes sense for things like food, yard waste, paper, and even some plastics. But for many things, including e-waste, the basic materials used to construct them can be hazardous. These materials will eventually be released. They can threaten water sources or later uses of the land if they escape the landfill. For this reason, many landfills in developed countries do not allow hazardous materials, including electronics.

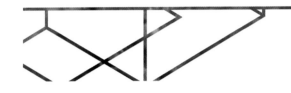

TCLP

In the toxicity characteristic leaching protocol (TCLP), materials such as electronic devices are ground up and then mixed with a fluid that contains acetic acid, a strong form of vinegar. This fluid is meant to simulate the water mixed with the chemical products of decomposition in a landfill. The mixture is then rotated in a drum for 18 hours, and the fluid is drained off and tested for the amounts of certain toxins. The EPA has set concentrations of toxins that are considered dangerous. For example, they have labeled levels of lead greater than 5 mg/L as hazardous.[2]

The EPA has a test called the toxicity characteristic leaching protocol (TCLP). It determines the dangers associated with materials in landfills. This test determines whether toxic compounds will seep out of the materials that contain them and into a landfill. Scientists performed the test on different devices, from laptops to remote controls, and found high concentrations of lead. Longer test periods of up to two years have shown that up to 0.07 ounces (2 g) of lead can leach from a computer motherboard.[1] Tests that realistically simulate landfill conditions also show that lead leaches out from computers into landfills.

INCINERATORS

Incinerators are another possible destination for waste in the United States. The plastics in e-waste could go to incinerators, but proper incineration requires high temperatures. Low-temperature burning, such as burning in the open air or even in low-temperature furnaces, can produce poisonous compounds such as dioxins. Dioxins are a group of chemicals with similar structures, and they accumulate in living tissues. They are poisonous and cause reproductive problems including fetal development issues. Even high-temperature industrial waste incinerators produce dangerous chemicals. They do have special equipment so these emissions can be removed before they enter the environment, but the emissions must still be collected and disposed of properly.

Incineration produces heat that is usually used to generate electricity. But incineration also produces carbon dioxide, a greenhouse gas, so it is not the ideal end point for e-waste or other plastics. Scientists agree releasing greenhouse gases into the atmosphere contributes to climate change. Incinerating waste is not common in the United States. The United States had 77 large incinerators in 2017, down from a peak of 187 in 1991.[3] Incinerators are controversial because they are expensive and produce greenhouse gases, toxic air emissions, and ash. There is a strong lobby in the United States

Taiwan had a population of 23.5 million in 2016.[4] It incinerates 96 percent of its municipal waste.[5]

26

against building new incinerators. Incineration is also not recycling. Many of the components of e-waste are lost after incineration. Incineration is more common in some countries in Europe and Asia.

RECYCLING E-WASTE

The EPA estimated that in 2010 Americans disposed of 1.79 million short tons (1.6 million metric tons) of electronic products, mostly in landfills. They recycled only 0.65 million short tons (0.59 metric tons) of e-waste that same year.[6] However, there have been reports that many devices collected for recycling are in fact exported out of the United States. The fate of these devices is not known, but presumably they were destined for informal recyclers.

Because of the risks involved in sending e-waste to landfills and incinerators, people send e-waste to recyclers. When e-waste is recycled, hazardous parts can be separated out so they do not harm the environment. Valuable parts can also be separated and reused.

In the United States, there are methods for safely recycling some e-waste. However, recycling is expensive, and the

WASTE INCINERATION

Waste incinerators are large furnaces that are fueled by burning waste in the presence of oxygen. They produce carbon dioxide, water, and ash as their main waste products. The ash is composed of everything that does not have carbon in it. This includes metals, glasses, and other mineral materials. Ash may include toxins such as heavy metals. Incinerators must be hot enough and the materials must remain in the furnace long enough to prevent the release of toxins that may form from incomplete combustion. Incomplete combustion occurs at low temperatures or with too little oxygen and produces molecules other than just carbon dioxide and water. The gases released from an incinerator are usually monitored and filtered, often with a fabric filter, to remove potential toxins. Spraying lime into the gases removes acidic gases that might form acid rain. Special incinerators are built to incinerate hazardous and medical waste. These incinerators have safer handling areas to feed waste into furnaces that guarantee complete burning and control emissions.

At Electronic Recyclers International in Massachusetts, United States, e-waste is broken down into smaller pieces and then shredded. Technicians then sort out parts such as plastics and metal.

process is slow. This is also the case in Europe and Asia. The technology is new and has not been expanded enough to handle the sheer amount of existing e-waste. For example, the United States does not have smelter facilities. Smelters recycle cathode-ray tubes (CRTs). So the United States sends CRTs to smelters in Canada and Europe. Recycling technology that recovers precious metals in other parts of e-waste is also currently too expensive to build. Because of this, most e-waste ends up in landfills, even though this comes with risks. And most e-waste destined to be recycled goes to informal plants in developing countries. There, the plants recycle e-waste, but they lack the proper technology to keep workers and the environment safe.

As awareness of informal recycling's hazards grows, China and India are researching new methods to effectively recycle e-waste. They recognize that in the near future most of the e-waste they receive will come from within their own borders. However, most recycling is still done informally. And of the total e-waste produced in the world, only an estimated 15 percent is completely recycled.[7]

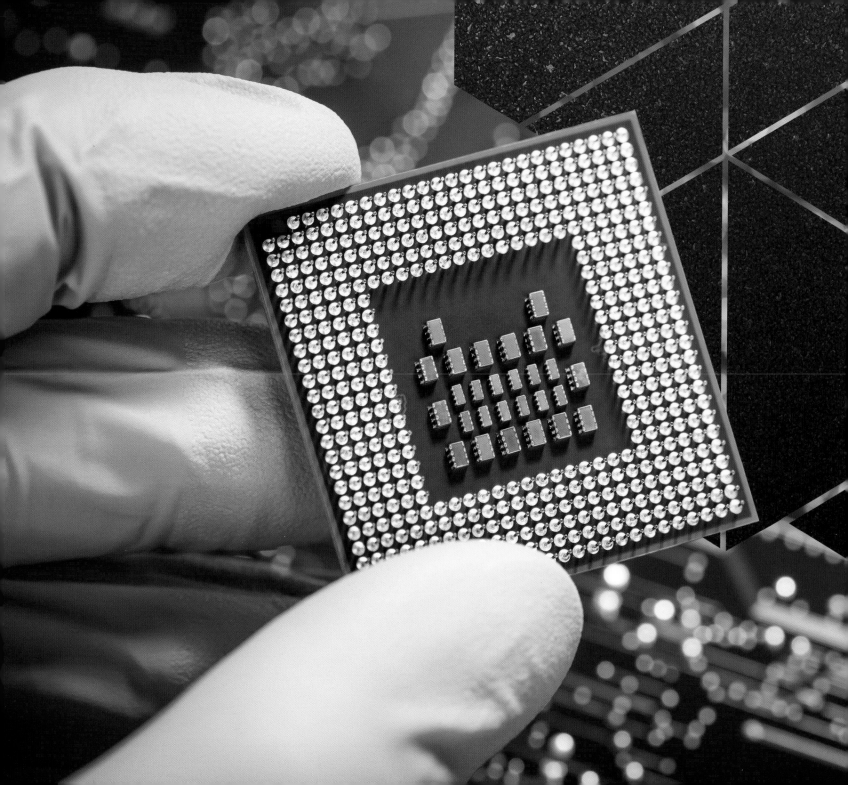

Chapter
FOUR

THE RISKS AND BENEFITS OF E-WASTE

O ne of the biggest challenges of recycling e-waste is separating the variety of materials used to make it. This variety is complicated by the way the different materials are mixed closely together. One simple example is wire. The

Each part of e-waste, from chips to capacitors, needs special technology to take it apart and sort the materials.

copper used in most wires is a valuable metal. But the wires are coated with plastic that insulates them to prevent short circuits. The plastic is tightly bound to the copper wire. In informal recycling, the plastic is sometimes burned to free the copper wire, but this creates toxins, including dioxins, lead, and soot. In more advanced recycling centers, the wire is shredded. The shredded material is scattered onto a vibrating table over which water flows. This floats off the plastic and leaves the copper behind. Other machines strip the plastic away from the metal wire, producing clean parts of copper and plastic. But that is only one piece of the puzzle. Taking a whole device, such as a laptop, and breaking it down into all of its individual components such as wire has its own challenges.

WEEE contains metals, plastics, glass, and many other materials. Parts such as batteries and printer cartridges house these materials. Each part's composition changes and will continue to change. Breakthroughs in technology will change the makeup of devices. New inventions will change the devices that people want to buy. Until recently, personal computers came with viewing screens made of heavy CRTs. These are the same screens that were used in old televisions. CRTs contain a variety of materials. They have valuable copper in their magnets' coils, but the heavy glass tube contains lead.

Technology is changing. Today, computer screens are no longer made with CRTs. They are either liquid crystal displays (LCDs) or LCDs with light-emitting diodes (LEDs) to

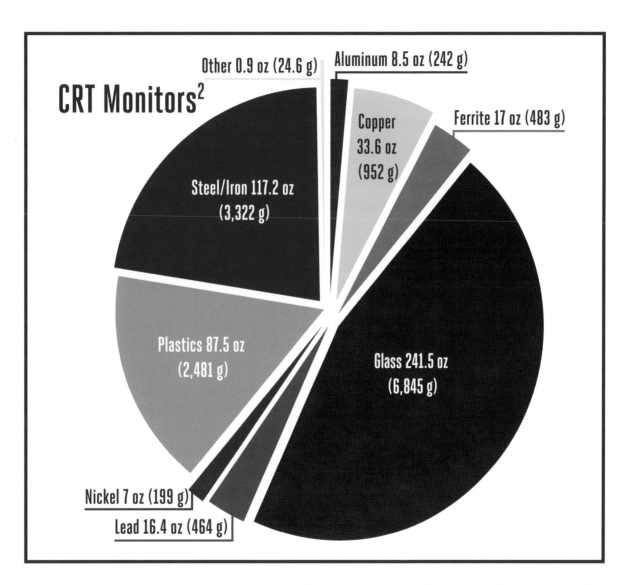

CRT Monitors[2]

- Other 0.9 oz (24.6 g)
- Aluminum 8.5 oz (242 g)
- Copper 33.6 oz (952 g)
- Ferrite 17 oz (483 g)
- Steel/Iron 117.2 oz (3,322 g)
- Glass 241.5 oz (6,845 g)
- Plastics 87.5 oz (2,481 g)
- Nickel 7 oz (199 g)
- Lead 16.4 oz (464 g)

This chart shows the materials that make up CRT monitors by weight. The most valuable materials take up only a small fraction of the weight. Gold accounts for 0.01 oz (0.31 g), and silver accounts for 0.04 oz (1.25 g).

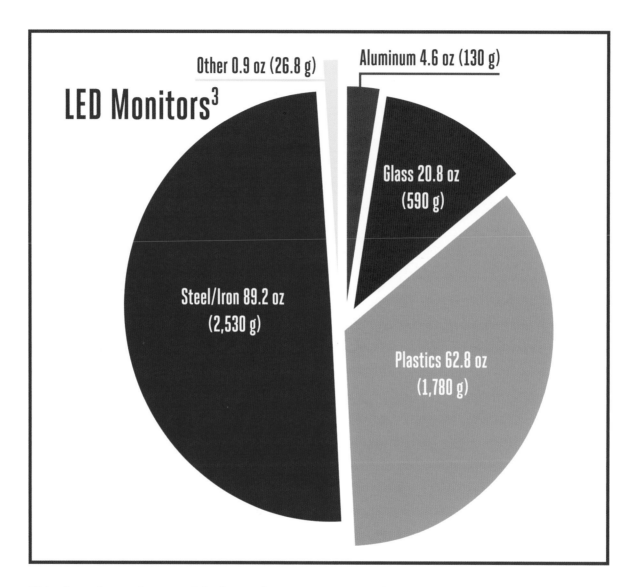

Other 0.9 oz (26.8 g)

Aluminum 4.6 oz (130 g)

LED Monitors[3]

Glass 20.8 oz (590 g)

Steel/Iron 89.2 oz (2,530 g)

Plastics 62.8 oz (1,780 g)

This chart shows the materials that make up LED monitors by weight. The devices contain several trace metals that make up a tiny percentage of the total weight, including cerium, europium, gold, indium, mercury, palladium, silver, and tin.

LCD screens create images by using one liquid crystal cell to act as one pixel in an image.

illuminate them. These screens contain different materials than those of CRTs and require different recycling methods. This makes recycling e-waste difficult. Technology changes rapidly, so new recycling methods and equipment need to change to keep up. At the same time, recyclers need to continue using older methods and equipment. Old technologies such as CRTs are expected to be a part of e-waste for several years to come as the old screens are removed from use. CRTs entering the waste stream have appeared to peak in the

The number of CRTs available for recycling is estimated to peak between 2015 and 2020.[5]

CRITICAL MATERIALS

Critical materials are raw materials important to the economy and at risk of disruptions in supply. Many critical materials belong to a group known as Rare Earth Elements (REEs). Found in the Earth's crust, these elements are difficult to mine because they do not occur by themselves in ores. REEs are not necessarily rare; they are just more difficult to mine. Examples are elements such as neodymium, which is used in magnets like those in headphones. Europium, terbium, and yttrium are used in LED and LCD screens. China produces approximately 85 percent of the world's rare earths.[8] This large production of rare earths in one country makes their supply vulnerable.

United States but could still be present in the waste stream until 2030.[4]

BREAKING DOWN E-WASTE

There are three major groups of materials in e-waste. By weight, steel and iron usually make up more than half of e-waste, followed by non-flame-retarded plastics, and then other metals.[6] The metals in e-waste can be divided into those that are valuable, such as copper, gold, and silver, and those that are dangerous for health and the environment, such as lead and chromium. Some metals are valuable because they are essential and their supply might be at risk. These are called critical materials. Critical materials include elements such as antimony, beryllium, and cerium. Some of the critical materials are also precious metals, such as platinum and palladium. There are also metals that are difficult to separate from the waste. For example, in recycling iron and steel, platinum and palladium that are mixed in cannot be recovered.

The plastics in WEEE are not as valuable as the metals, but many can be recycled—and they can pose threats when they are burned improperly or put into landfills. Plastics make up between 11 and 30 percent of WEEE's weight.[7] The exact amount depends on the devices. Plastics themselves need to be separated into two groups: those with flame retardants added to make them less dangerous in a fire and those without flame retardants.

HOW VALUABLE IS E-WASTE?

The value of the materials in e-waste changes depending on demand and supply. Although most metals are present in only small amounts in electronics, the value of some of the metals and other materials can make their recovery worthwhile. Yet due to the expense of safely recycling e-waste, many developed countries do not recycle most of their e-waste. Much of it goes to informal recyclers who do not have the ability to safely recycle e-waste. Without safety equipment, they collect the valuable materials from e-waste at the cost of damage to the environment and their own health.

AVERAGE PRICES FOR SOME METALS IN 2015[9]

METAL	PRICE
Aluminum	$0.88/lb ($1.94/kg)
Copper	$2.77/lb ($6.10/kg)
Gallium	$133.80/lb ($295/kg)
Germanium	$530.70/lb ($1,170/kg)
Gold	$17,055/lb ($37,600/kg)
Indium	$209/lb ($460/kg)
Nickel	$5.73/lb ($12.64/kg)
Palladium	$10,070/lb ($22,200/kg)
Platinum	$15,740/lb ($34,700/kg)
Silver	$233/lb ($514/kg)
Zinc	$0.95/lb ($2.09/kg)

Burning the plastic around copper wire releases toxins into the air, where they can harm not only plants and animals, but also the people who work and live in the area.

FIVE

ENVIRONMENTAL POLLUTION AND E-WASTE

While e-waste has many valuable parts, it is also dangerous. These dangers are magnified when e-waste is recycled informally. Most recycled e-waste is recycled at informal plants. Because of a lack of regulation and safety equipment, workers involved in informal recycling of e-waste do not have a way to deal with the hazardous parts of e-waste. Instead, dangerous chemicals are released into the environment when workers burn parts in open air and dump chemicals in fields or streams. When these chemicals are present in the environment, they harm plants and animals. Especially in areas where pollutants already stress ecosystems, e-waste chemicals can make it more likely for species to become locally extinct. But there is a second reason to be concerned about these chemicals in the environment. Chemicals in the environment affect people's health.

Chemicals that are dangerous to ecosystems usually have three characteristics. The first is that they are toxic in some way. Toxins can work quickly or over longer periods of time. Quick toxins, or acute toxins, usually damage cells and cause organ damage, which leads to illness and sometimes death. Toxins that work over long periods are called chronic toxins. Carcinogenic toxins cause cancer. Other chronic toxins cause birth defects or affect proper growth. Chronic toxins may affect a person or animal's reproductive system, making the individual less fertile or even infertile.

The second characteristic of chemicals dangerous to ecosystems is that they are persistent. Many chemicals are broken down by environmental conditions and living organisms, especially by bacteria. A persistent chemical remains in the environment for long periods of time. Elements such as metals are persistent because they cannot be broken down into anything smaller that might be less harmful. Elements are as simple as any chemical can be because they are made up of only one kind of atom.

Unlike elements, molecules can be broken down into the atoms they are made of. But they can still be persistent if they do not get involved in chemical reactions easily. If a chemical does not react easily, it is difficult for an organism's body to break it into pieces that are less toxic.

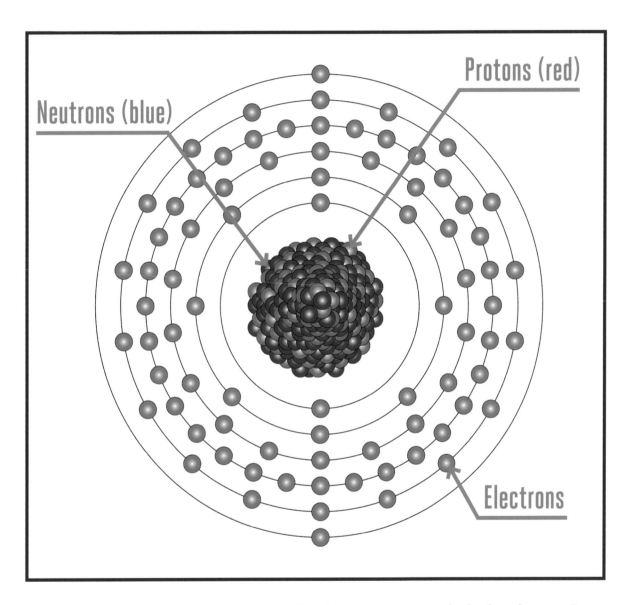

The mercury atom is the smallest thing the element mercury can be broken down to. Some mercury atoms are made of 80 electrons, 80 protons, and 122 neutrons.

Finally, many chemicals increase in concentration in living organisms, making them more dangerous to ecosystems than other chemicals. Many of these chemicals have low concentrations in water, soil, and air. But when they are measured in the plants and animals living in these environments, the concentrations are much higher. This is called bioaccumulation. A living thing's exposure to chemicals in the environment may not make it sick. But if the chemical is able to bioaccumulate, it can reach toxic levels in the organism. Chemicals that bioaccumulate usually also biomagnify. This describes what happens to the chemical in a food chain. When the chemical is measured in species from the bottom to the top of a food chain, the concentrations biomagnify, or increase, the higher up on the food chain the species is. This happens because herbivores eat many individual plants to survive. Then predators eat those herbivores, and top predators eat many other predators. Each level of the food chain gets higher and higher doses of the contaminant from its food source.

BIOACCUMULATION

Most chemicals can be divided between those that dissolve in water and those that dissolve in oils and fats. Both types can be toxic. The types that dissolve in oil can be more of a problem for living things because they are stored by the body in fat, where they accumulate. Health consequences for the organism can occur when the fat is used for energy and the toxins are released all at once. Many substances that bioaccumulate will also biomagnify. Substances that bioaccumulate and biomagnify tend to be persistent chemicals, meaning that the organisms that take them in cannot break them down in their bodies.

THE MAIN CONTAMINANTS: METALS

Metals make up a large part of e-waste. The most valuable substances in e-waste are metals, but many metals are both not valuable and difficult to remove. These often end up being discarded. The most important metals from an environmental standpoint are the heavy metals. Heavy metals are toxic.

They also bioaccumulate and biomagnify. The heavy metals that cause the most health risks are lead, mercury, cadmium, chromium, and arsenic.

Lead is an additive to glass in CRTs. In CRTs, the glass that faces the user, panel glass, is lead-free. But the funnel and neck of the CRT contain lead. The lead will eventually leach out of the glass if it is put in a landfill, so this is not a preferred solution. The funnel glass can be sent to a smelter to separate out the lead. At the smelter, the glass is melted and the lead removed. The glass portion is then landfilled or used as filler in construction materials and pavement. This is the process used in Japan, but in less developed countries, the funnel glass usually ends up in landfills. In North America, there are few smelters available to carry out the work. In the developing world, the procedures are not environmentally friendly. In the United Kingdom and the United States, a new commercial process separates the lead from funnel glass using a closed electric furnace. While promising, the capacity of these furnaces is still small, and the cost of the process requires that customers pay to have their CRTs recycled.

Lead is also a part of the solder in older circuit boards. Solder is a metal with a low melting point. It is used to connect electric components. Lead is also found in fluorescent

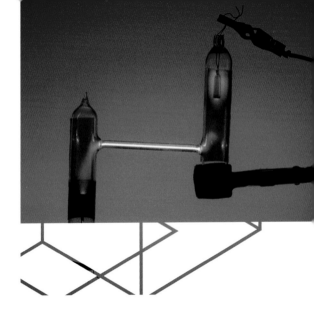

LEAD IN CRTS

The lead in the glass of a CRT, pictured above, is concentrated in the funnel and not in the face panel, the part facing the viewer. There is also lead in the material that joins the face panel to the funnel. The purpose of the lead was to shield people from exposure to the harmful X-rays produced in a CRT. A 26-inch (66 cm) television with CRTs contains approximately 5 pounds (2.27 kg) of lead in its glass. A 17-inch (43 cm) computer monitor with CRTs contains approximately 2 pounds (1 kg) of lead in its glass.[1]

lamps and batteries. High lead concentrations can cause brain damage, kidney damage, and damage to the digestive system.

Mercury is a metal found in fluorescent lamps and other types of lamps, though less and less is being used. Mercury causes cell damage and will affect many organ systems in the body. Cadmium is found in many components including batteries, pigments, printed circuits, and plastics. Cadmium can cause cancer, damage organs, and cause nervous system effects.

Chromium is present in printed circuit boards and plastics. Certain chromium compounds are strong cancer-causing agents and will also cause liver and kidney damage. Arsenic is present in LCD displays. Certain forms of arsenic cause severe damage to cells and therefore will damage many different organ systems. Arsenic also appears to cause cancer.

The glass in LCDs contains significant amounts of arsenic. This glass also contains indium, a rare and expensive metal. A few methods can extract this material, but no one has managed to develop large-scale recycling methods yet. Today, most LCD screens are lit with LEDs. These screens have similar toxins as regular LCD screens, but with two additions: LEDs also contain the rare elements germanium and gallium.

HEAVY METALS

Heavy metals are very dense. While some heavy metals are essential nutrients people need in their diets, such as copper, zinc, and chromium, most are not used by living things. Most heavy metals are toxic in high concentrations, even the essential nutrients. In addition to being toxic, most heavy metals also bioaccumulate and biomagnify. The most toxic heavy metals are arsenic, cadmium, chromium, lead, and mercury. Each of these is present in e-waste parts in some amount.

Heavy metals enter the environment in several ways during informal recycling. The acid baths used to separate precious metals are discarded onto soil or into waterways. These baths contain heavy metals such as lead and arsenic. E-waste that has been processed is typically dumped nearby on land or in waterways, where metals can leach out of the waste into the environment. The dust from informal e-waste processing contaminates the air with heavy metals.

THE MAIN CONTAMINANTS: ORGANIC COMPOUNDS

Organic compounds are molecules that contain carbon and hydrogen. The dangerous forms of these compounds usually have chlorine, bromine, or fluorine atoms in their structures. Other dangerous forms have an aromatic ring, a ring structure of atoms in the molecule that can make it less reactive. Many of these compounds are dangerous because they are persistent and biomagnify. Some are the most toxic compounds known to humans.

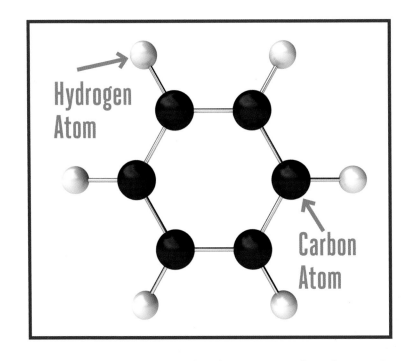

Benzene molecules are examples of aromatic ring structures.

SMELTING

Smelting is one process that makes metals. It is often used to make copper from ore, which is rock that contains copper combined with other elements. Mined ores or recycled materials containing copper are crushed, separated by particle size, and the particles containing the metal are sent to a smelter. The refined ore or recycled material is fed into a smelter where the material is heated to a temperature above 2,200 degrees Fahrenheit (1,200°C).[2] The furnace produces a molten mass that separates into slag and matte. The slag is waste. The matte consists of liquid copper sulfide, iron sulfide, and other metals, including precious metals if they are present.

The matte is drained out of the furnace. Sometimes air is blown through it, causing air to react with the sulfur to separate it from the matte, forming slag. The slag is removed, leaving behind blister copper, which is approximately 97 or 98.5 percent pure copper.[3]

The blister copper is then refined through electrolysis. Electrolysis is a process of forcing a chemical reaction using an electric current. In electrolysis, an anode and a cathode are submerged in a solution. On an industrial scale, the anode is a large slab of blister copper. The cathode is a thin strip of highly purified copper. A voltage is applied across the anode and cathode. This breaks the copper in the anode into positively charged ions, which are atoms with a charge, and two electrons. The ions and electrons travel to the cathode, where they combine again, making pure copper. In the process, the impurities in the anode also dissolve. Some of these, which include precious metals, fall to the bottom of the tank and can be removed. Others, such as zinc and arsenic, stay in the solution and are removed later. By the end of the process, which takes a couple of weeks, the cathode consists of copper that is 99.9 percent pure. This copper is pure enough for most applications, such as producing wire.[4]

ELECTROLYSIS

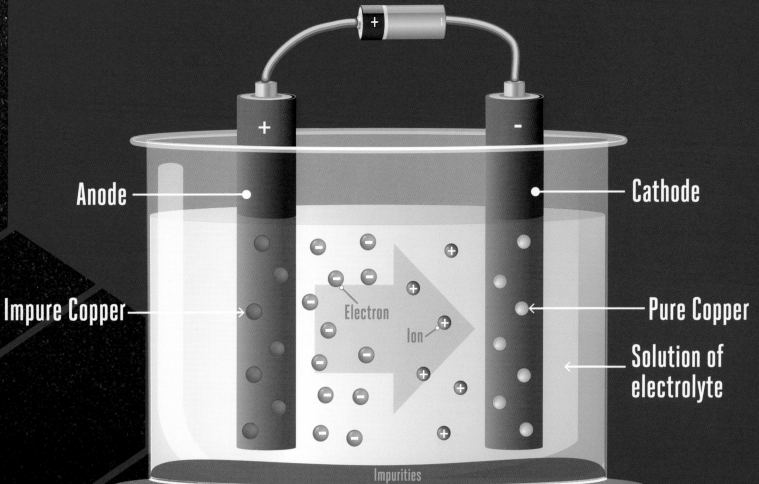

Anode

Cathode

Impure Copper

Pure Copper

Electron

Ion

Solution of electrolyte

Impurities

Polychlorinated biphenyls (PCBs) are persistent, and they biomagnify. PCBs are found in older electrical components such as transformers. They have been banned for most uses since the 1980s. There are many kinds of PCBs, and the effect of each type varies. PCBs have been found to be neurotoxins and hormone mimics. Neurotoxins interfere with the proper functioning of the nervous system. Hormone mimics imitate hormones, which control body functions including sleep, appetite, growth, and reproduction. When hormones arrive at a target tissue, the hormone binds like a key in a lock with a molecule on the surface of cells, causing changes in the cell that bring about the desired effect. Hormone mimics attach to the molecules in the body that hormones normally attach to, making it seem like hormone levels are higher than they should be, or preventing hormones

The Lianjiang River, which runs through Guiyu, has high levels of heavy metals.

49

from attaching, making it seem like the levels are too low. The body reacts to the higher or lower levels, causing health issues such as infertility and cancer. PCBs also have immune system effects and cause cancer.

Flame retardants are added to plastics and fabrics to reduce their ability to burn. They are found in many of the plastics present in e-waste, including wire coatings, the board part of a printed circuit board, and plastic coverings such as the outside of a computer monitor. Some flame retardants are organic molecules that contain bromine or chlorine. Other forms contain phosphorus, and there are some that contain both phosphorus and chlorine or bromine. Many older flame retardants, especially those containing bromine, are persistent and may cause health effects, so they are no longer used. Yet many of their replacements are also persistent and have various short- and long-term toxic effects. Most flame retardants are not actually chemically bonded to the plastics with which they are combined, so they come out of the plastic easily.

Almost every person has flame retardant molecules that can be measured in his or her body because the molecules are present in so many products.[5] Research into the safety of flame retardants continues, but many are known to cause health risks. The toxicity of flame retardants depends on the exact

THE PROBLEM WITH HORMONE MIMICS

Hormones are produced by glands in the body in carefully controlled amounts, and they move through the blood stream to many tissues throughout the body. The problem with hormone mimics is there is nothing controlling the amounts of a hormone mimic in the body. Hormone mimics can result in sterility or reduced fertility, brain damage, and defects in developing embryos in animals. In humans they have been linked to delayed sexual maturation in boys, breast cancer in women, and prostate cancer.

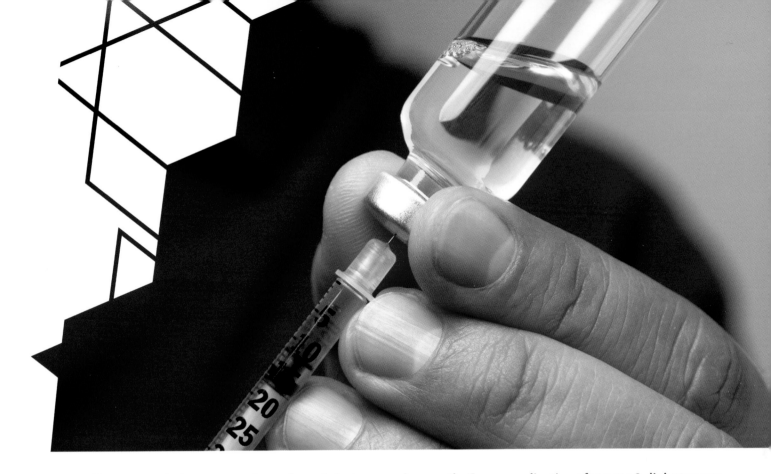

Hormone mimics are not always harmful when used correctly. Some medications for type 2 diabetes use hormone mimics to cause the body to produce insulin.

type, and there are many. Some mimic hormones. Others are potential carcinogens, and still others have been shown to affect brain development.

Today, if plastics with flame retardants do not end up in landfills, many are incinerated to produce energy. This solution is less ideal than recycling because it produces greenhouse gases. And rules set in place in Europe in 2006 make it impossible to sell

The US Centers for Disease Control and Prevention believes there is no safe level for lead in children, as even low levels of lead have been shown to affect IQ, attention, and academic achievement.

recycled plastics containing brominated flame retardants. Technology that can separate plastics with flame retardants is still in development.

Finally, there are organic compounds that are produced by burning. Burning plastics with flame retardants produces dioxins and dibenzofurans, which are persistent, biomagnify, and are extremely toxic. They have similar chemical structures to dioxins. Burning plastics also produces polycyclic aromatic hydrocarbons (PAHs). These compounds can be carcinogenic, cause developmental abnormalities, and suppress the immune system.

CONTAMINANTS IN THE ENVIRONMENT

These toxins make their way from informal recycling plants into the environment. Scientists have studied the environments around some informal e-waste recycling plants. Soil and streams around Guiyu have high levels of toxic chemicals. For some of these compounds, levels were almost three times higher than levels expected to have an effect on wildlife. Many of the sites contained higher-than-normal levels of heavy metals.[6]

Also in Guiyu, researchers found high levels of PCBs in plants from farm fields and soils near processing areas. They also found flame retardant compounds in plants, including vegetables, and the soil. A study of flame retardants and dioxins in Guiyu found the highest measured levels in soils underneath processing areas. River sediments and fish in Guiyu's river also have flame retardant compounds. Sediment concentrations are ten to 1,000 times higher than measurements made in other polluted sites. Concentrations in tilapia and bighead carp were tens to thousands of times higher in Guiyu than in tilapia or similar fish species measured from unpolluted and polluted locations elsewhere.[7]

Another processing location, Taizhou, China, had high concentrations of dioxins, PCBs, and PAHs in farm field soils near the processing site. The soils around processing areas also had high concentrations of these chemicals. Rice samples in Taizhou had levels of lead that were 3.4 times higher than acceptable levels under Chinese regulations, and the soils also had high levels of arsenic, cadmium, chromium, mercury, and other metals.[8]

Outside of China, in a study of an informal e-waste recycling site in Bangalore, India, scientists measured concentrations of metals in the soil outside of the recycling buildings. They found much higher levels of lead in some of the samples than is recommended by the EPA. Informal recycling also takes place in Agbogbloshie, a suburb of Accra, Ghana. Researchers took several soil samples from areas where wires were burned to remove plastic. They also took

FLAME RETARDANT LAWS

The goal of flame retardants is to make homes safer in the event of a fire. However, it appears the compounds used actually make homes less safe in another way. Many flame retardants produce toxic chemicals when they burn, which is especially dangerous for firefighters, who are around fires often. Some states and countries are trying to reduce the use of flame retardants, and some people lead protests to get companies to remove flame retardants from products. As of 2016, 13 states have banned the sale of some kinds of flame retardants for certain products. Seven other states have proposed similar laws.[9] California now requires labeling on products containing flame retardants. The European Union has banned certain types of flame retardants, and a few manufacturers have removed flame retardants from their products.

In Guiyu, some acid baths were located near the river. Acid was sometimes dumped in the river after use.

soil samples near the river by the town. Both sets of samples had high levels of lead. The levels exceeded the EPA standards for soil by as much as 15 times.[10]

CONTAMINANTS IN WILDLIFE

Toxins are also present in wildlife around informal e-waste recycling plants. A study in Fengjiang, China, measured the amount of PCBs and flame retardant compounds in snails. They compared the levels in the snails with the level in the soil. They found the compounds bioaccumulated in the snails. Lead in snails decreased farther away from the recycling site, showing that the site was the source of the toxins.

Chinese scientists also studied the levels of contaminants in waterbirds. The study was conducted in an area of Zhejiang Province where informal e-waste recycling occurs. The researchers found high levels

Cattle graze contaminated land in Agbogbloshie. Toxins leach into the ground and can cause animals to become sick.

The Chinese pond heron had the highest contamination levels in a Chinese study because it feeds mostly on fish, which carried more toxins than the insects and seeds the other birds ate.

of PCBs in the birds. They also found that several newer flame retardants biomagnify. The levels were higher in birds that were higher on the food chain, such as the Chinese pond heron and white-breasted waterhen, and lower in the ruddy-breasted crake, which is lower on the food chain.

In Qingyuan County, China, researchers studied toxin levels in chickens and ducks near an e-waste processing area. Chickens living closer to the e-waste processing site had higher levels of flame retardants in their bodies. The scientists suggested that domestic chickens might be a major source of flame retardant contamination for humans.

All of these results have raised awareness of how informal recycling contributes to severe pollution in the areas around the recycling businesses. Pollution with these types of chemicals is typical of the industrial pollution that occurred in the past in developed countries, which now reduce pollution through laws that put limits on the release of pollutants into the air, water, and soil. At the informal recycling sites, because many of the pollutants are persistent in the environment, they will remain there and gradually affect species farther and farther away from the recycling site. In addition, when people from the area eat vegetables grown in the contaminated soils or eat animals grazing nearby or the fish from the local rivers, they will concentrate the contaminants in their bodies.

Formal recycling workers have clothing and tools that keep them and the environment safe from e-waste toxins.

SIX

HEALTH EFFECTS OF INFORMAL RECYCLING

In many countries, governments create regulations that protect workers at their jobs. Many jobs are dangerous by their nature or could be dangerous if not carried out in a safe way. Toxins released into the environment by informal recycling harm workers and people who live near those sites. This is why government regulations in countries including the United States require business owners to protect their workers' safety. However, many countries do not have these regulations, or they do not enforce them. In addition, unsafe activities in informal businesses may not be visible to governments, making them hard to regulate. But studies are raising awareness of the dangers involved.

MEASURING THE DAMAGE

Scientists have made two kinds of studies to measure how dangerous the work is. In the first type of study, scientists measure the quantities of different known toxic substances in the bodies of workers and people who live near the workplace, including the children and families of the workers. Many toxic substances have known safe levels that can be compared to the amounts found in different tissues in a worker's body. These comparisons measure how much risk a toxin poses to a worker. However, these studies do not show how the health of the worker is being affected.

The study that measures toxin levels in workers is simple to carry out, and there have been many studies done in different recycling locations around the world. Most of the studies have been done in China, especially by the laboratory of Dr. Xia Huo, a toxicologist at the Shantou University Medical College.

The other type of study looks for actual health problems in workers who have toxins present in their tissues. These studies provide stronger evidence that the workers' exposure to e-waste is damaging their health. However, they are more difficult to perform because many health effects take long periods of time to occur, and the effect of the toxin must be somehow separated from other possible causes.

Children in Guiyu played and worked among the e-waste, exposing themselves to many toxic chemicals.

STUDIES IN GUIYU

Guiyu has been at the center of many studies on informal recycling. Researchers found high frequencies of skin damage, headaches, vertigo, nausea, chronic stomach pain, and ulcers in Guiyan workers. From 2004 to 2008, Dr. Huo found that Guiyan kindergarteners had blood chromium levels two to three times higher than levels in a similar group from a town that had no e-waste recycling.[1] The higher chromium levels affected Guiyan

TOXICOLOGIST

A toxicologist studies how people and other species take in poisons and what effects those poisons have on them. Dr. Xia Huo is an environmental toxicologist. She studies how poisons in environments such as workplaces affect workers and their families. Toxicology research is important for identifying chemicals that are dangerous to people and wildlife. The research is also important for deciding which levels of toxins should be allowed in the environment to maintain safe homes, workplaces, and natural habitats.

children's growth. Newborns had high levels of chromium and higher-than-normal damage to their DNA.

Dr. Huo's lab studied chromium levels in newborns' umbilical cord blood from 2006 to 2007 in Guiyu. This is an easy location to obtain blood that shows which chemicals are in the blood of the newborn. The lab found that chromium levels were higher in babies whose mothers were involved with e-waste recycling. They also found more DNA damage in the white blood cells of newborns who had higher chromium levels. The DNA damage may lead to greater chances of cancer.

Over four years, Dr. Huo's lab also studied chromium levels in children's blood in Guiyu and then took physical measurements of the children to look for differences that suggested the chromium was affecting the children's growth. The study found higher levels of chromium in the children from the e-waste site compared to the levels in children from a nearby town. They also found higher levels of chromium in children who had higher body weight and greater physical growth. The study authors suggest that these changes are a result of the chromium.

Studies have also measured blood lead levels in Guiyan children. Researchers found in 2004 that blood lead levels were higher in Guiyu compared to those in a non-e-waste site.

They found that 82 percent of the Guiyan children had levels higher than twice the level considered acceptable by the US Centers for Disease Control and Prevention.[2] Studies also found that blood lead levels increased with the age of the child. By 2011 to 2013, the same researchers still found high blood lead levels in children in Guiyu, but they were lower than in 2003. They suggest that some attempts since 2003 by researchers to make the e-waste work safer for children had been successful. Other researchers connected high blood lead levels with lower IQ and school performance in children.[3]

In a study of a new flame retardant, Dechlorane Plus, Chinese researchers found levels in the blood of workers in Guiyu to be three times higher than those in a comparison group that did not participate in e-waste recycling. The amounts were higher than ever reported in wildlife or humans. The health effects of Dechlorane Plus are unknown.

STUDIES OUTSIDE GUIYU

While Guiyu was a common center for research, it is not the only informal recycling area studied. In 2014, scientists measured levels of PAHs in the bodies of e-waste workers in

TOXICITY

How do scientists discover if something is poisonous? It would be unethical to feed people poisons to find out how much would make them sick. With many chemicals, there have been accidental poisonings that give some information about how toxic something is. Most of the information we have about toxins comes from their effects on other animals. Scientists use rats to estimate how toxic most chemicals would be to people. Rats are similar enough to people that they give helpful information. Scientists can study rats to learn about acute toxicity, or how deadly a chemical is, and to determine a poison's long-term effects. Many substances are first tested for their ability to cause cancer. Scientists determine this by the amount of DNA damage a poison causes in bacteria.

Longtang Town, Qingyuan City, China, and also measured levels of two chemicals that indicate DNA damage. The levels of PAHs were higher than levels in non-e-waste workers. The levels of DNA damage were also higher. But the scientists could not prove that the increase in DNA damage was from the PAHs.

Scientists studied amounts of PCBs and flame retardants in the blood of e-waste workers in a recycling site located in northern China. They compared the workers with a group near Tianjin, China, that did not work with e-waste. While both groups had the toxins in their blood, the e-waste workers' concentrations were 1.5 to 7.4 times higher.[4] Workers in Guiyu had not shown PCB contamination, so different types of e-waste may have been processed there.

People are exposed to lead through inhalation, ingestion, or physical contact. The workers in Guiyu were exposed to lead in all three ways.

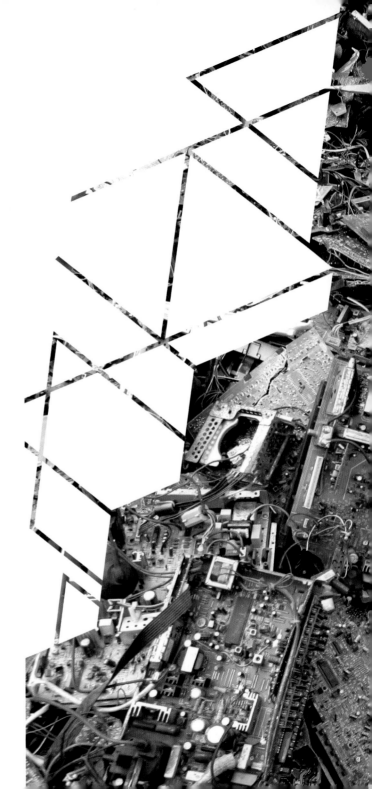

MEASURING LEAD IN BLOOD

Scientists take blood to measure how much lead is in a person. They can measure lead with a few different methods. For each method, scientists must be careful to not contaminate a sample with the lead that is still in the environment today.

One method, called atomic absorption spectrometry, uses light to measure lead. First, the blood sample, including any lead it contains, is vaporized. This is done either with a flame or in an electrically heated furnace made of graphite. All elements absorb light of certain wavelengths. This amount is unique to an element. Scientists send a wavelength that lead absorbs into the blood sample. They measure the amount of light absorbed. This tells scientists how much lead is in the blood.

The flame method is easy to perform and inexpensive, but it is not able to detect small concentrations of lead.

One of the most precise methods is called inductively coupled plasma mass spectrometry. This method strips electrons from atoms using extremely high heat. The process produces atoms with the same charge. Researchers can compare the charge to the mass of each atom to identify the element to which atoms belong. This method is expensive and requires some skill to use, but it can detect low amounts of lead, and it can measure several elements at the same time from a small sample.

An atomic absorption spectrometry machine can detect lead and other metals in blood, but it can only look for one metal at

RESEARCHING BIRTH RECORDS

Birth records are the information a hospital records when a baby is born. They include things like whether the child was born before the expected date and the newborn's weight and size. In the United States, these records include more than one hundred pieces of information that can help public health scientists understand what might affect the health of a newborn. These include a mother's illnesses, whether the mother smokes, the newborn's behavior, and any of the newborn's physical abnormalities. All of these things can be related to the newborn's health and can alert public health scientists to hidden health problems that may be present in the population.

There have been fewer studies on the effects of e-waste recycling outside of China. Researchers studied the levels of PAHs in the bodies of workers in Agbogbloshie, Ghana, and found them to be higher than levels in a comparison group that did not work at the e-waste site.

MEASURING ACTUAL HEALTH EFFECTS

All of these studies proved people who informally recycled e-waste had dangerous levels of toxins in their bodies. But studies have also linked exposure to e-waste toxins with health effects. From 2001 to 2008, Dr. Huo's lab studied birth records from Guiyu and a similar area that did not have e-waste recycling. The study showed higher miscarriage rates in Guiyu, a higher percentage of low birth weight in babies, and more babies born before full term. All of these results are indicators that mothers and their developing fetuses were in poorer health in the e-waste recycling area than they were where recycling did not take place. Other studies of birth outcomes in e-waste recycling areas have shown that levels of various toxins such as PAHs, PCBs, and flame retardants in the mother are related to miscarriages, low birth rate, and premature births.

A study of children in Guiyu showed that high blood levels of chromium and nickel affected the health of the children's lungs. It restricted the volume of air the children were able to exhale. Children with high blood levels of the metals manganese and nickel weighed less and were shorter than children with lower levels.

A pair of research studies also looked at the mental health of children in Guiyu. The studies found that children with higher blood lead levels were less adaptable to new situations, tended to withdraw from new experiences, and had higher activity or fussiness levels. Tests on newborns' reflexes and responses also showed lower scores when they had higher levels of lead in their blood. The researchers "concluded that neonates [newborns] in Guiyu who were exposed to higher lead levels due to the recycling of e-waste may have impaired neural behavior."[5]

These studies are early signs that informal e-waste recycling has potentially serious health effects on the people doing the work. The evidence gives reason enough to develop methods to safely recycle in countries that rely on informal recycling. If countries improve the safety of e-waste recycling in developing countries, workers can keep their jobs and have fewer risks to their health.

The rate of miscarriages in Guiyu is four times the rate in a nearby control area not involved in e-waste processing.[6] The rate in the control area was about the same as the rate in the United States.[7]

Chapter
SEVEN

RECYCLING
POLICIES

Guiyu continued as a busy hub for electronics recycling until the summer of 2015, when families began leaving the town for two reasons. Prices for metals and plastics produced by the recycling had been declining, making the work less profitable. And the government asked businesses to move their workplaces to a new industrial park being built near the town. On December 1, 2015, the government

The industrial park in Guiyu marked China's new efforts to enforce laws banning the import of hazardous waste. Since much of the e-waste at Guiyu was imported, the mounds of electronics disappeared, as did many workers.

ordered the remaining 3,000 workshops in Guiyu to move into the industrial park, or the power would be cut off to the shops and the workers might be arrested.[1] When journalists visited Guiyu near the end of December, there were no longer any informal recycling operations in Guiyu. The piles of electronics to be recycled had all disappeared. Approximately 3,000 formerly family-run businesses had merged into 49 new businesses that occupied the new industrial park. The size of the recycling business in Guiyu had been an $800 million (US) per year business processing 1.8 million short tons (1.6 million metric tons) of e-waste.[2] In mid-2016, it shrunk to processing 441,000 short tons (400,000 metric tons).[3]

The smaller volume of work in the industrial park appears to be safer for the workers. However, researchers do not know where the millions of tons of waste that were recycled in Guiyu go now. The waste may have moved to another informal recycler. The fate of the migrant workers who made a small living in Guiyu has also not been reported. Did they find employment at another informal recycling area? Were they able to find employment at all? Eliminating health risks in Guiyu is a step forward by the Chinese government in dealing with the huge problem of e-waste in China and around the world, but it is only a beginning.

RECYCLING BY REUSE

E-waste can be recycled in different ways. At the top of the list is reuse. In many parts of the world, the electronic devices discarded by wealthy nations can have a second life as useful devices in less wealthy nations. People can also reuse parts. An e-waste recycling site in Agbogbloshie, Ghana, harvests useful parts from many devices, including computers and phones. The harvesting must be done by hand and is time-consuming. Then technicians use the parts to repair or build new devices. These new devices can then be sold by the recycling company. In Africa, this is an important source of computers. For many discarded devices, however, there is no longer any reuse value. The only value is in the raw materials from which they are made.

THE BASEL CONVENTION

China is following the lead of other countries that regulate recycling to protect workers and the environment. But one of the biggest challenges is having rules and programs in place that make sure electronic devices are recycled safely and do not end up in landfills. This is a surprisingly difficult task, but there are a growing number of places that are attempting to make these rules. Some of these laws work. Others do not.

An early global attempt to regulate e-waste began in 1992. An international agreement called the Basel Convention made it illegal under international law to ship hazardous waste across international borders. Most countries in the world have signed onto it. The United States is the only major country to not have ratified the agreement, as the government would first need to make laws to fulfill the convention's requirements. According to the agreement, e-waste is hazardous waste because of the dangerous materials used to make it. The intention of the agreement is to avoid the possibility of wealthy countries shipping an expensive problem to poorer countries where people suffer the health and environmental consequences. Under the agreement, countries need written agreement from the receiving country and cannot export if they believe the e-waste will not be processed responsibly. According to the EPA, the purpose of the convention is "to promote environmentally sound management of exported and imported waste, especially in developing countries."[4]

But the Basel Convention has been poorly enforced. Countries can classify e-waste as devices for reuse, and the countries receiving the e-waste do not prevent it from crossing their borders. In a 1996 response to lobbying efforts, the Basel Ban Amendment was adopted. It specifically banned exports of hazardous waste from certain developed countries to developing countries. The ban has not yet been enacted because not enough countries have signed onto it. This is just one of several ineffective regulations that attempt to solve the hazards of informal recycling.

LAWS IN CHINA

Some countries are working to reduce informal recycling within their own borders. China has made attempts to develop e-waste recycling systems that are safe, but it has met with little success. The difficulty in China is that any formal e-waste recycling system must compete with the informal system. This informal system depends on countless small-business scrap dealers that might consist of only one family. However, an attempt was made in nine cities to stimulate recycling by offering a 10 percent discount on new appliances if the old one was recycled. The program was quite successful and allowed more than 46 million old appliances to be recycled in formal recycling centers.[5] Other attempts at recycling e-waste have been less successful. In China, it is common practice to sell waste electronics to street collectors, and these collectors pass

BASEL CONVENTION

The Basel Convention is named for Basel, Switzerland, where the treaty convention was first held in 1989. The treaty took effect in 1992. A total of 185 countries have signed the agreement.[6] All of those countries have ratified or made it the law in their own countries, except the United States and Haiti. The Basel Convention's definition of hazardous waste included e-waste because of the many toxic materials present in it.

China's new appliance discount sent more e-waste to formal recycling operations, where regulations kept workers safer.

the devices on to informal recyclers. The street collectors generally pay more than formal recyclers for obsolete devices, so it is difficult for formal recyclers to obtain enough material to recycle.

China is also becoming more serious about enforcing its laws on the treatment of e-waste. These efforts led to the closing of businesses in Guiyu. However, this will reduce the problem only in China. The stricter controls in China are likely to shift the movements of e-waste to the other countries with fewer regulations.

LAWS IN INDIA

India, like China, has a large informal recycling sector. As much as 95 percent of India's e-waste is recycled informally.[7] India developed e-waste laws in 2012, but the laws have

E-waste pollution has taken its toll on communities in India. Near Bangalore, the ground emits flammable gas because of the nearby landfill, where natural waste and e-waste have leached toxins into the ground.

had little effect so far. The laws require manufacturers and sellers of electronic equipment to develop take-back systems for their devices and to inform the buyers about their options when the device becomes obsolete. As in China, however, it is difficult for formal recyclers to compete with informal recycling businesses. As of 2015, few manufacturers and sellers had developed take-back programs, and few electronics consumers knew what they could do with their devices when they became obsolete.

Even if the laws had worked, they did not address the loss of livelihood for the informal recyclers. Some experiments have tried to solve that problem by encouraging existing informal e-waste collectors to enter the formal recycling market. In Bangalore, local businesses that produced e-waste were convinced to send it to a

STATE E-WASTE RECYCLING LAWS[9]

KEY
STATES WITH E-WASTE LAWS

Twenty-eight states passed e-waste recycling laws between 2003 to 2016.

formal recycling system operated by former informal workers. Attempts are being made to reproduce this approach in other cities. These approaches are encouraging, but the path to eliminating dangerous recycling practices in India will be a long one.

LAWS IN THE UNITED STATES

Some countries enact laws to try to reduce the amount of e-waste sent to other countries for informal recycling. In the United States, there are no federal regulations on recycling e-waste. Instead, 28 states and the District of Columbia have laws that regulate e-waste.[8] Some are more effective than others. Two of the first laws were in California and Texas.

Since its e-waste recycling laws were passed in 2003, the volume of e-waste collected in California and recycled appropriately has increased to a stable amount of just under 200 million pounds (90 million kg) per year.[11]

California led the way in 2003. It made it illegal to throw electronic equipment away with regular trash. Laws limit the amount of cadmium, chromium, lead, and mercury in electronic devices sold in the state. California stores must collect a recycling fee from customers who buy electronic devices. The fee pays for the collection and recycling of e-waste. Consumers must bring their waste electronics to an authorized recycler. Recyclers are required to report their activities, including what they did to the e-waste and where they shipped any recycled materials.

A 2007 law in Texas followed suit. It requires each company that makes computers sold in Texas to provide a free recycling program for buyers. Each company must report every year on the weight of computers collected for recycle and reuse in the program, but this is the only information required. A similar program was established for televisions in 2011. The laws require recyclers to handle the computers and televisions in accordance with all laws, but recyclers do not have to officially report their activities. The fate of the collected devices is unknown.

THE RIGHT INCENTIVE

One way states try to reduce e-waste is by making companies that make the products pay. Until recently, companies have not been required to pay for damage done to the environment. Instead, older models ended up in landfills paid for by taxpayers. Some of the

Some cities hold a recycling day, when people can bring electronics to be recycled.

new laws about e-waste are intended to make companies pay this cost. If the laws work, one outcome will be that products will last longer or be easier to repair or recycle.

According to the University of Pennsylvania, rules in 23 states require the makers of electronic products to cover the cost of collecting and recycling them.[10] The goal is to encourage manufacturers to make greener products. Greener products are less expensive to recycle or more likely to be repaired or reused. This has also been the goal of other take-back programs, such as those in Europe and Canada.

There are two ways that companies typically pay for recycling. One is called collective producer responsibility (CPR) and the other is called individual producer responsibility (IPR),

> **"Our research finds that Individual Producer Responsibility (IPR) is a better incentive for design change. . . . Experience from manufacturers of electrical and electronic equipment and automobiles in both Japan and Sweden shows that such systems have resulted in design change."[12]**
>
> *—2006 report commissioned by Greenpeace International, Friends of the Earth Europe, and the European Environmental Bureau*

or extended producer responsibility. In CPR, rules apply to a whole group of companies that make one type of product, such as computers. People return computers for recycling. Each company owes a certain amount of money to cover the recycling based on how many computers it sold. The problem with this system is that if a company makes a greener product, one that is cheaper to recycle, it still pays the same share as the other companies. Since the company's recycling costs do not decrease if it makes a greener computer, it has no financial incentive to make the greener computer. Most systems in the United States work this way.

The IPR approach requires each individual company to take back and recycle its own computers. In this system, if a company makes an improvement that makes a computer easier to recycle, the company benefits from that improvement because it costs less.

There is a drawback to the IPR system. It must be possible to identify each company's products in the waste to enforce the rules, and this is sometimes expensive. If it is expensive to identify each company's products, then the recycling program will be too expensive for manufacturers. There are some places where this problem has been solved. Maine requires each company that sells an electronic product in the state to be registered, which helps this identification process. Because of this, each company's products can be identified in the recycled materials. This affects how much companies are charged.

There is a final problem with how recycling is paid for. In most of Canada and in California, a fee is charged for each device purchased by a consumer, so the manufacturers are not responsible for paying for recycling. In other states, the manufacturer pays the fee for each device sold, but there is no rule saying it cannot add to the cost of the product, recouping its fee from the consumer. Thus, neither system makes the manufacturing company pay for what happens to its products at the end of their lives. Even if an IPR system was being used, because the consumer ends up paying the actual cost of recycling, companies are not encouraged to make greener products.

MAKING EFFECTIVE LAWS

Some e-waste laws are ineffective because they do not provide the right incentive. The University of Pennsylvania presented guidelines to help make recycling laws more effective. First, laws should define what e-waste is; otherwise, many devices will not be considered e-waste, and consumers will not recycle them. They should also allow recycling of as many different devices as possible, which encourages people to recycle all of the e-waste they have at home. For example, keyboards and computer mice are not considered waste in most of the states with e-waste recycling laws, including California. Second, the laws should encourage collection in rural as well as urban areas, or the rural devices will not be collected. Third, the laws should ban e-waste from landfills. All of these approaches increase the volume of e-waste that is available and make recycling more profitable for the businesses doing the recycling. Finally, the

In 2014, only 15 US states had bans on disposing of e-waste in landfills.[13]

E-WASTE CRIMINAL

In March 2013, the owner of a Michigan recycling company was sentenced to 2.5 years in prison, and the company was fined $2 million. The charges were trafficking in counterfeit goods and breaking environmental laws. The recycler had created false factory stickers on old CRT tubes so they could be sold to Egypt, which prohibits imports more than five years old. Over five years, the recycler exported approximately 100,000 old CRTs to Egypt.[14] Also in 2013, a Colorado company was convicted of exporting CRTs to countries, including China, while falsely claiming to clients that the CRTs would be recycled safely in the United States.[15]

laws should encourage reuse before recycling by providing a credit for reusing a device.

Although state regulations help the situation, federal laws are needed. States cannot enforce rules about exporting e-waste. Only the federal government can. Exporting is what feeds informal recycling. Having one set of federal rules instead of 28 state rules would also make it easier and less expensive for manufacturers to comply. Presently the EPA does not allow hazardous waste to be sent to other countries. Aside from CRTs, the federal government does not consider e-waste hazardous, so there is no US law preventing its export to other countries.

MAKING SAFE RECYCLING POSSIBLE

One of the biggest reasons very little e-waste is recycled in the United States is because of its expense. The equipment needed to safely recycle e-waste is expensive or has not been developed. A recycling company needs to have enough e-waste to make up the money spent on equipment. But there are very few recycling companies in the United States, so people have trouble finding where they can recycle e-waste. Most of this e-waste ends up in storage or landfills. There is not enough e-waste for a formal recycling company to make a profit. If most of the waste

One reason recycling e-waste is expensive is because there is not enough of it being collected for recycling. When there is a greater supply, the price will go down.

goes to landfills or is exported or stored by its owners, then there is not enough to make recycling worthwhile. As Chase Hinsey, a recycler in Texas, says, "There is a profit, but until you get volume, it's difficult to make money in this market."[16]

State laws help break this cycle. Because of state laws, e-waste collection is becoming much more efficient, and this increases the amounts of e-waste available for processing. Another promising development is that, while only 15 states have laws banning e-waste landfill disposal or incineration, companies are working to address the lack of technology to handle e-waste.[17]

Chapter
EIGHT

E-WASTE RECYCLING TECHNOLOGY

Technology plays a vital role in safely recycling e-waste. Developed countries do not have enough facilities and technology in place to recycle e-waste cheaply, efficiently, and safely. So they export it to countries such as China and

Some electronic recycling collection events have volunteers to help people unload large devices.

India, which produce millions of tons of e-waste themselves. Developed countries are also trying to create safe recycling methods, and one important piece of the puzzle is technology that keeps their workers safe.

E-WASTE RECYCLING IN THE UNITED STATES

The United States does not recycle most of its e-waste, but the e-waste it does recycle requires complex technology in order to recycle safely. The first step in e-waste recycling in the United States is collecting the devices. How this is accomplished depends on the state and the type of device. In some cases, the manufacturer collects the material through mail-back programs. In other cases, city governments, private businesses, or nonprofit agencies coordinate the take-back effort. Some electronics stores in the United States offer a take-back program.

A worker takes apart a television at a recycling center in Indianapolis, Indiana.

86

ROBOTIC DISMANTLING

Dismantling electronic devices is an essential step in recycling because it allows the most valuable materials to be concentrated. It also removes impurities that can make recovering those valuable materials difficult. One reason some consider informal recycling economically practical is because of the cheap labor. Cheap labor is generally not available in developed countries. Apple Inc. has developed a robot that is able to dismantle an iPhone 6s in 11 seconds. The robot, called Liam, is a large assembly-line machine with a total of 29 arms that remove various parts of the phone and save each. Some of the components may be reused, while others will be sold to materials recyclers. Liam, which was unveiled in 2016, will be able to dismantle 1.2 million iPhones in a year, and Apple is designing new machines to dismantle other products.[2] But Liam currently cannot handle the number of devices that need to be recycled. And manufacturers less wealthy than Apple may be unable to follow with their own systems.

After collection, the e-waste must be sorted and dismantled. In this step, different types of devices may be separated. Often, taking apart the devices is accomplished by hand. However, it is also possible to shred whole devices such as cell phones. Taking apart a device produces streams of e-waste that are as pure as they can be. For example, all of the glass, plastics, large metal components, and hazardous parts should be separated. When this sorting has taken place, the different groups of e-waste have more value because fewer different treatments are needed to extract the desired raw materials.

How devices are dismantled can affect how much of a valuable material can be recovered. For example, if phones are shredded, the amount of gold recovered is 11.3 oz/short ton (354 g/metric ton). However, if the circuit boards are removed by hand, the amount of gold recovered is 31.4 oz/short ton (982 g/metric ton).[1]

Two different methods can be used to recover the metals from sorted e-waste. Smelting is the main method used to recover metals from e-waste. Hydrometallurgy uses low temperatures with chemicals dissolved in water to dissolve and collect metals from e-waste. It is becoming more commonly used, but the products of hydrometallurgy are often hazardous and must be treated carefully.

Smelters are located in Belgium, Austria, Spain, Sweden, and Canada. Smaller smelters are located in Japan and South Korea. There are no smelters in the United States, so e-waste needs to be shipped to a country with a smelter. Smelting melts the copper out of e-waste as well as the metals that are able to dissolve in liquid copper such as silver, gold, and platinum. After smelting, copper can be purified further and the precious metals removed, leaving pure copper and bricks of mixed precious metals such as gold, silver, platinum, and palladium.

During smelting, the plastics that have not been removed from the e-waste are burned in the furnace and provide a source of energy to help melt the metals. However, burning plastics in a smelter means toxins are produced, and the gases emitted by the furnace must be treated to prevent their escape.

A method still being developed through research is called biometallurgical processing. These processes use bacteria, algae, or fungi that interact with metals, such as by absorbing them, to remove metals from e-waste. The metals can then be purified from the microorganisms that contain them. One benefit of these processes will be that they do not use strong acids to remove metals, making it easier to dispose of the final waste products.

A final method of removing the metals from e-waste is hydrometallurgy. Usually the e-waste is shredded and ground so the chemicals can attack the materials more easily.

BIOMETALLURGY

Using living organisms to extract metals from e-waste is not as farfetched as it sounds. In fact, mining companies have used bacteria to remove metals from ores since the late 1950s. There are two processes in which living organisms can be used to remove metals from complex mixtures: bioleaching and biosorption. Bioleaching is used by the mining industry to treat ores and waste materials to remove metals. The metals on which bioleaching works best are copper, cobalt, nickel, zinc, and uranium. These metals are bonded to sulfur. The organisms remove the sulfur from the metal, releasing it in a soluble form. The organisms that do this are acid-loving bacteria and archaea. Bacteria and archaea are two groups of single-celled organisms. E-waste recyclers want to extract precious metals such as gold from e-waste. Gold does not form compounds with sulfur, but this method can still be useful. The organisms help by removing the other metals that contaminate the gold.

This method is also being used to clean up contaminated soils and sediments. Research in bioleaching e-waste continues. Scientists are trying to find organisms that will specifically extract precious metals.

Biosorption uses living organisms such as algae, bacteria, and fungi, whose cell surfaces stick to precious metals. The work using biosorption has been mostly experimental, but biosorption has been used to extract gold from solutions. The only biosorption test done on e-waste used the method to remove metals from e-waste leachate. It also used biosorption as one step in a process to remove other metals. Using biosorption in that step showed promise, but this process for removing precious metals from e-waste is some time away from being used in recycling plants.

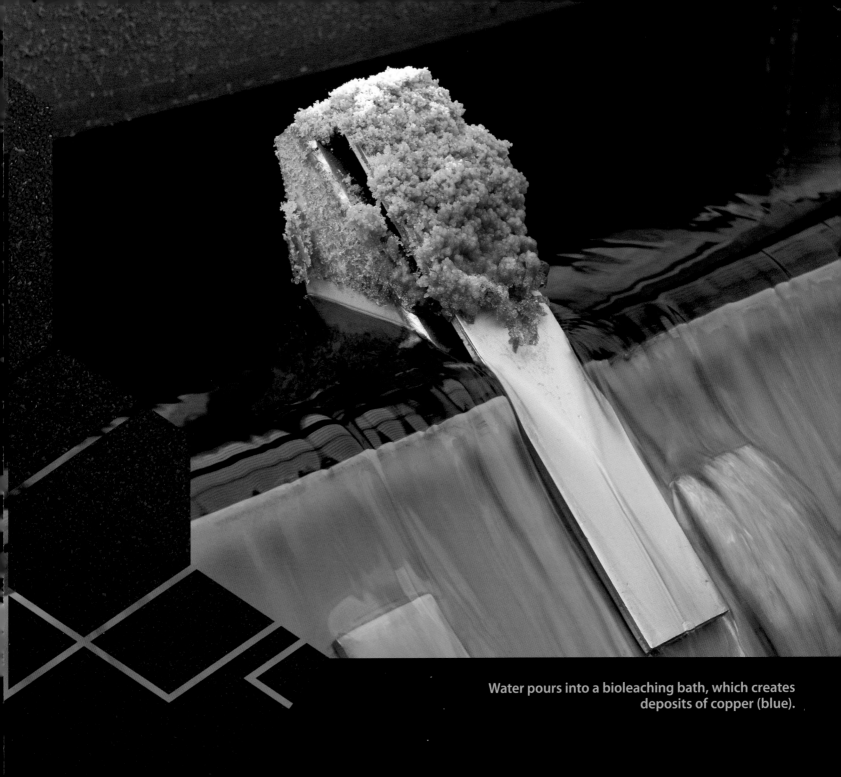

Water pours into a bioleaching bath, which creates deposits of copper (blue).

A series of acids are used to dissolve different metals from the e-waste. Once the metals are removed from the e-waste, they can be separated from the solution by passing an electric current through it or by evaporating the liquid part of the solution.

The technology of hydrometallurgy is not developed enough to process large quantities of e-waste. But some people are finding ways to collect different parts of the waste using this process. ATMI, a US business, developed a process to extract useful parts like chips, gold, and other metals from printed circuit boards using hydrometallurgy. The process is being developed by international corporation Entegris, which bought ATMI in 2014.

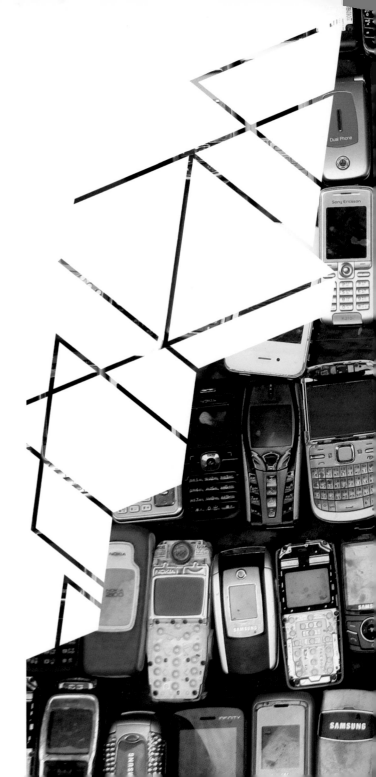

People in countries including Thailand gather and sell old phones for profit.

REUSE

There is economic sense in reusing electronics versus recycling them, at least while they are still usable. The sale price of a used computer or cell phone is far higher than the value of the materials in it that can be recycled. The sale price of a refurbished device is even higher. This means that an original owner, a refurbishing company, or a broker of used devices has the potential to extract more value from the device than a recycler does.

Refurbishing, selling a used device, and recycling all involve costs that take away from each of these values. But the value for the processor is much higher for refurbished and used devices than it is for recycled. To improve the availability of reused devices, information about repairing devices must be more freely available. Methods of destroying personal information stored on devices must also be easier to use and more thorough, so there is less risk to the first owner.

THE THREE RS

Laws, rapidly changing electronics technologies, and expenses all keep countries from safely recycling e-waste. Some countries are working to fix this. But there is something individuals can do as well. There are different approaches to dealing with e-waste in the United States depending on where a person lives. However, one approach works anywhere. People can conserve. Conservation is a response to the throwaway society. It considers three Rs—Reduce, Reuse, Recycle—that help cut back on waste.

The first R is reduce. Reducing means consuming less. By reducing, people conserve by curbing the number of devices made. This may mean not buying as many luxury devices. It also means keeping items in use for as long as they work regardless of what new products may appear on the market. The consumer should consider keeping an older electronic device that still works. Many devices that are thrown away still do the job they were intended to do. Even if an upgraded model can do more, the updates are often unnecessary. The old device will serve its owner just fine until it breaks.

VALUES FOR REFURBISHED, USED, OR RECYCLED DEVICES IN 2010 AND 2011.[3]

DEVICE	TYPE	REFURBISHED	USED	RECYCLED
PHONE	Android	$145	$122	⟨$2
	iPhone	$180	$203	$1
LAPTOP	PC (15 in)	$450	$359	$17
	Apple (15 in)	$700	$600	$18

People can make the most money off of a refurbished device, as the device as a whole is more valuable than the materials that make it.

There are two sets of standards that e-waste recycling companies can use to be certified, proving they are recycling responsibly. One is called Responsible Recycling, or R2, which was developed by Sustainable Electronics Recycling International, and the other is e-Stewards, developed by Basel Action Network.

If the reduce option has been exhausted, the next step is to consider the reuse option. Reusing means repairing products that are broken so they can continue to be used. Consider researching repair options before discarding a broken device. This information can be found through the manufacturer or local electronics repair shops. The performance of some devices may also improve with upgraded parts. A computer's performance often improves using this approach. Upgrades in software or hardware can also improve a device. Another way to reuse is to give or sell the device to someone else. Many consumers look for inexpensive devices and are not concerned about how new they are. Options for reuse include selling the electronics online or donating them to a facility that will try to resell them before directing them to a recycling stream.

Finally, if there is no way to continue to use or reuse a device, then the device can be recycled. This stage, while conserving resources, uses more resources than the other two steps. It takes energy to recycle and remake products from the raw materials obtained from recycling. Recycling is also never 100 percent effective. Materials are lost along the way, and many materials, such as paper and plastic, cannot be recycled indefinitely. They eventually reach a point at which they must end up in a landfill.

If recycling is necessary, the EPA provides online information resources for recycling e-waste. Those resources include state-specific options and information by manufacturer

Software and hardware updates can both improve the performance of a device and prolong its life by making it more secure from attacks.

and retail outlet for companies that have take-back programs. Your city or town should also have online or in-person resources available to assist with directing e-waste to a recycler. Recycling is also important because recyclers depend on volume to make their businesses profitable. As more people start to recycle their e-waste, more e-waste recycling options will become available. Recyclers will be able to make a profit on recycling e-waste. This will reduce the amount of harm e-waste causes to people and the environment. It will also encourage the invention of new technologies and processes that make recycling safer and more affordable to people who recycle without any safety precautions.

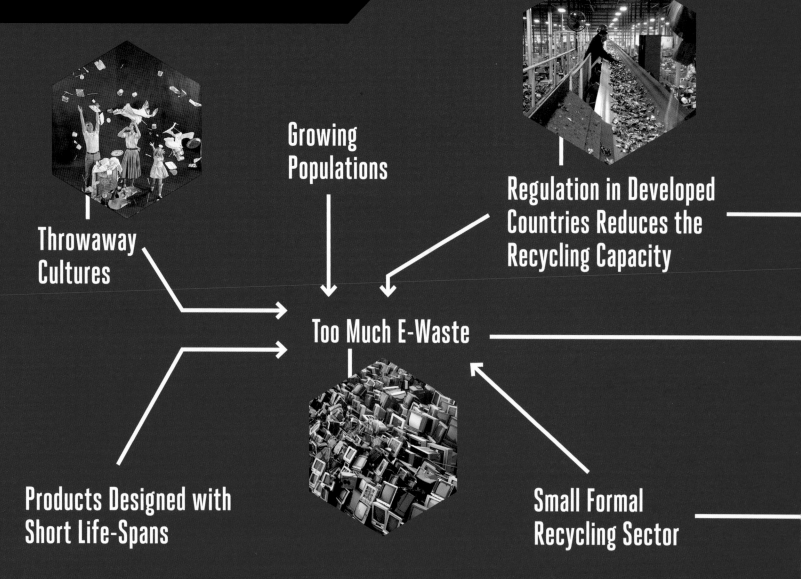

Throwaway
Cultures

Growing
Populations

Regulation in Developed
Countries Reduces the
Recycling Capacity

Too Much E-Waste

Products Designed with
Short Life-Spans

Small Formal
Recycling Sector

Low Wages and
Low Employment in
Developing Countries

Environmental
Contamination

E-Waste Shipped to
Informal Recyclers

Worker Health Damage

Poor Safety
Regulations
in Developing
Countries

ESSENTIAL FACTS

WHAT IS HAPPENING

Tens of millions of tons of electronic devices are discarded each year. Many are sent to landfills or are being exported to developing countries where they are recycled for their valuable metal content by informal businesses. The informal recycling exposes the environment and the workers to dangerous levels of toxins present in the e-waste.

THE CAUSES

The primary cause is the overconsumption of electronic devices, which are designed with short life-spans. Countries do not have the technology or capacity to safely recycle the amount of e-waste that is being produced. Because informal recyclers have few choices for employment that provides a steady income, they choose to work with unhealthy e-waste recycling processes.

WHEN AND WHERE IT'S HAPPENING

E-waste is produced throughout the world, but the United States, China, and Europe are the largest producers. The e-waste is mostly recycled in China, western Africa, Southeast Asia, and India. Informal recycling has probably been happening since the 1980s and is still happening today.

KEY PLAYERS

» Developing nations have had poor regulations that allow e-waste to be imported and domestic e-waste to be processed unsafely. Developed nations have been reluctant to develop safe recycling methods for their e-waste.

» Throwaway societies discard electronics before they have broken or replace working devices with upgraded models, adding to the amount of e-waste produced each year.

» Companies that make electronics regularly release upgraded models in response to throwaway societies that want new gadgets. Companies make the products with short life-spans so that people have to buy the products more frequently, and the products are no easier to recycle.

WHAT IT MEANS FOR THE FUTURE

Informal e-waste recycling has contaminated many sites with toxic wastes. Many people's health has been damaged, and individuals will continue to become ill from working at recycling e-waste. Both developed and developing nations must work together to create methods for safe recycling and to protect the health of workers and the environment.

QUOTE

"There is a profit, but until you get volume, it's difficult to make money in this market."

—Chase Hinsey, Innovative Electronics Recycling

GLOSSARY

bioaccumulation

The increase or buildup of a substance, such as a toxin, in the body of living organisms.

biomagnification

The increase in concentration of a contaminant in the bodies of organisms higher up a food chain.

cathode-ray tube (CRT)

A closed tube of glass in which a beam of high energy electrons is directed in a vacuum toward a screen containing a substance that lights up when exposed to radiation.

diode

An electronic device that uses two electrodes to turn an electric current that regularly changes directions into a constant electric current that only flows in one direction.

dioxin

A chemical compound produced during combustion of some organic compounds that is one of the most toxic molecules known to science.

economy

A system in which things are ranked by value and exchanged.

electronic

Containing an electric circuit with control devices such as transistors and diodes.

element

A substance that is made up of only one kind of atom and cannot be broken down into simpler substances by ordinary chemical means.

flame retardant

A chemical added to plastics, textiles, and other products to reduce their flammability.

greenhouse gas

A gas that absorbs infrared radiation and traps heat in the atmosphere.

heavy metal

A metal with a high atomic weight, generally found in the middle of the periodic table, that is often toxic.

molecule

The smallest unit into which a substance can be broken down that is made of two or more atoms and has all of the same properties of the original substance.

PAH

Polycyclic aromatic hydrocarbon, a class of chemicals made up of two or more aromatic rings produced by combustion of organic materials.

PCB

Polychlorinated biphenyl, a group of chemicals consisting of two aromatic rings with varying numbers of chlorine atoms attached; PCBs are no longer manufactured.

refurbish

To make better or fix by replacing old parts with new parts.

smelt

To extract a metal from its ore using a process of heating and melting.

soluble

Capable of being dissolved in a liquid.

toxin

A poison.

ADDITIONAL RESOURCES

SELECTED BIBLIOGRAPHY

"Global E-Waste Volume Hits New Peak in 2014: UNU Report." *United Nations University*. United Nations University, 20 Apr. 2015. Web. 9 Jan. 2017.

Minter, Adam. *Junkyard Planet: Travels in the Billion-Dollar Trash Trade*. New York: Bloomsbury, 2013. Print.

Spaul, Jon. "World's Biggest E-dump, or Vital Supplies for Ghana?" *SciDev.Net*. SciDev.Net, 10 May 2015. Web. 10 Jan. 2017.

Standaert, Michael. "China's Notorious E-Waste Village Disappears Almost Overnight." *Bloomberg BNA*. Bloomberg BNA, 17 Dec. 2015. Web. 10 Jan. 2017.

FURTHER READINGS

Bow, James. *Electrical Engineering and the Science of Circuits*. Saint Catharines, ON: Crabtree, 2013.

Green, Dan. *The Elements*. New York: Scholastic, 2012.

Thompson, Tamara. *What Is the Impact of E-Waste?* Detroit, MI: Greenhaven, 2011.

WEBSITES

To learn more about Ecological Disasters, visit **abdobooklinks.com**. These links are routinely monitored and updated to provide the most current information available.

FOR MORE INFORMATION

For more information on this subject, contact or visit the following organizations:

Basel Action Network

206 First Avenue S., Suite #410
Seattle, WA 98104
206-652-5555
http://www.ban.org

A nongovernmental organization that researches and lobbies to prevent e-waste from damaging the environment or workers.

Solving the E-waste Problem (STEP)

Step Initiative, UNU-IAS SCYCLE, UN Campus
Platz der Vereinten Nationen 1
53113 Bonn
Germany
+49 0 228 815 0214
http://www.step-initiative.org

An international organization, part of the United Nations University, that researches the e-waste problem and seeks possible solutions to it.

SOURCE NOTES

CHAPTER 1. A HEALTH AND ENVIRONMENTAL DISASTER

1. Xia Huo, et al. "Elevated Blood Lead Levels of Children in Guiyu, an Electronic Waste Recycling Town in China." *Environmental Health Perspectives* 115.7 (2007): 1113–1117. *ResearchGate*. Web. 3 Feb. 2017.

2. Pi Guo, et al. "Blood Lead Levels and Associated Factors among Children in Guiyu of China: A Population-Based Study." *Plos One*. PLOS, 19 Aug. 2014. Web. 3 Feb. 2017.

3. Xijin Xu, et al. "Birth Outcomes Related to Informal E-Waste Recycling in Guiyu, China." *Reproductive Toxicology* 33.1 (2012): 94–98. *ResearchGate*. Web. 3 Feb. 2017.

4. "Computer History 101: The Development of the PC." *Tom's Hardware*. Purch Group, 23 Aug. 2011. Web. 3 Feb. 2017.

5. C. P. Baldé, et al. "The Global E-Waste Monitor—2014." Bonn, Germany: United Nations University, IAS – SCYCLE, 2015. *United Nations University*. Web. 3 Feb. 2017.

CHAPTER 2. WHAT IS E-WASTE?

1. "Advancing Sustainable Materials Management: Facts and Figures Report." *EPA*. US Environmental Protection Agency, 2013. Web. 3 Feb. 2017.

2. Tim Cooper. "Slower Consumption Reflections on Product Life Spans and the 'Throwaway Society.'" *Journal of Industrial Ecology* 9.1–2 (Jan. 2005): 51–67. Print.

3. "Throwaway Living: Dozens of Disposable Housewares Eliminate the Chores of Cleaning Up." *Life* 39.5 (1 Aug. 1955): 43–44. Print.

4. Callie W. Babbitt, et al. "Evolution of Product Lifespan and Implications for Environmental Assessment and Management: A Case Study of Personal Computers in Higher Education." *Environmental Science and Technology*, 43.13 (2009): 5106–5112. *ResearchGate*. Web. 3 Feb. 2017.

5. Susanna Ala-Kurikka. "Lifespan of Consumer Electronics Is Getting Shorter, Study Finds." *The Guardian*. The Guardian, 3 Mar.

6. Rachel Courtland. "Gordon Moore: The Man Whose Name Means Progress." *IEEE Spectrum*. IEEE, 30 Mar. 2015. Web. 3 Feb. 2017.

7. C. P. Baldé, et al. "The Global E-Waste Monitor—2014." Bonn, Germany: United Nations University, IAS – SCYCLE, 2015. *STEP*. Web. 3 Feb. 2017.

8. Ibid.

9. Ibid.

10. Ibid.

11. Ibid.

12. Camston Wrather. "Quantitative GHG Reduction Using Micron Thermal Separation and Green Chemistry." *Solve*. MIT Center for Collective Intelligence, 2016. Web. 3 Feb. 2017.

13. "Copper Recycling." *European Copper Institute*. European Copper Institute, 2017. Web. 3 Feb. 2017.

CHAPTER 3. HOW E-WASTE IS MANAGED TODAY

1. Yadong Li, et al. "Dynamic Leaching Test of Personal Computer Components." *Journal of Hazardous Materials* 171 (2009): 1058–1065. *rmu.edu*. Web. 3 Feb. 2017.

2. Valerie J. Brown. "Hazardous Waste: Electronics, Lead, and Landfills." *Environmental Health Perspectives* 112.13 (Sept. 2004): A734. *ResearchGate*. Web. 3 Feb. 2017.

3. "Incineration and Incinerators-in-Disguise." *Energy Justice Network*. Energy Justice Network, n.d. Web. 3 Feb 2017.

4. "The World Factbook: Taiwan." *Central Intelligence Agency*. Central Intelligence Agency, 12 Jan. 2017. Web. 3 Feb. 2017.

5. Jill Chin. "Waste in Asia." *Responsible Research 2010: Issues for Responsible Investors* (Mar. 2011): 4–88. *sustainalytics.com*. Web. 3 Feb. 2017.

6. "Electronics Waste Management in the United States through 2009." *EPA*. US Environmental Protection Agency, May 2011. Web. 3 Feb. 2017.

7. Michelle Heacock, et al. "E-Waste and Harm to Vulnerable Populations: A Growing Global Problem." *Environmental Health Perspectives* 124.5 (May 2016): 550–555. *National Institute of Environmental Health Sciences*. Web. 3 Feb. 2017.

CHAPTER 4. THE RISKS AND BENEFITS OF E-WASTE

1. Aimin Chen, et al. "Developmental Neurotoxicants in E-Waste: An Emerging Health Concern." *Environmental Health Perspectives* 119 (2011): 431. *National Institute of Environmental Health Sciences*. Web. 3 Feb. 2017.

2. Federica Cucchiella, et al. "Recycling of WEEEs: An Economic Assessment of Present and Future E-Waste Streams." *Renewable and Sustainable Energy Reviews* 51 (Apr. 2015): 263–272. *ResearchGate*. Web. 3 Feb. 2017.

3. Ibid.

4. "An Analysis of the Demand for CRT Glass Processing in the U.S.A." *Chicago Bridge and Iron Company*, Aug. 2013. *Kuusakoski Recycling*. Web. 3 Feb. 2017.

5. Julia R. Mueller. "Direction of CRT Waste Glass Processing: Electronics Recycling Industry Communication." *Waste Management* 32.8 (2012): 1560–1565. *ResearchGate*. Web. 3 Feb. 2017.

6. Rolf Widmer, et al. "Global Perspectives on E-Waste." *Environmental Impact Assessment Review* 25.5 (2005): 436–458. *ewasteguide.info*. Web. 3 Feb. 2017.

7. Jef R. Peeters, et al. "Closed Loop Recycling of Plastics Containing Flame Retardants." *Resources Conservation and Recycling* 84 (2014): 35–43. *ResearchGate*. Web. 3 Feb. 2017.

8. Allison Carnegie. *Power Plays: How International Institutions Reshape Coercive Diplomacy*. New York: Cambridge UP, 2015. 25.

9. "Commodity Statistics and Information." *USGS*. US Geological Survey, 19 Dec. 2016. Web. 3 Feb. 2017.

CHAPTER 5. ENVIRONMENTAL POLLUTION AND E-WASTE

1. A. Monchamp, et al. "Cathode-Ray Tube Manufacturing and Recycling: Analysis of Industry Survey." *Electronic Industries Alliance* (2001). *eiae.org*. Web. 3 Feb. 2017.

2. "Processes: Copper Mining and Production." *European Copper Institute*. European Copper Institute, 2017. Web. 3 Feb. 2017.

3. "Primary Copper Smelting." *EPA*. US Environmental Protection Agency, 27 Sept. 2016. Web. 3 Feb. 2017.

4. Ibid.

5. Ronald A. Hites. "Polybrominated Diphenyl Ethers in the Environment and in People: A Meta-Analysis of Concentrations." *Environmental Science and Technology* 38.4 (2004): 945–956. *ACS Publications*. Web. 3 Feb. 2017.

6. Anna Leung, Zong Wei Cai, and Ming Hung Wong. "Environmental Contamination from Electronic Waste Recycling at Guiyu, Southeast China." *Journal of Material Cycles and Waste Management* 8.1 (Mar. 2006): 21–33. *ResearchGate*. Web. 3 Feb. 2017.

7. Qian Luo, Zong Wei Cai, and Ming Hung Wong. "Polybrominated Diphenyl Ethers in Fish and Sediment from River Polluted by Electronic Waste." *Science of The Total Environment* 383.1–3 (Oct. 2007): 115–127. *ResearchGate*. Web. 3 Feb. 2017.

8. Jianjie Fu, et al. "High Levels of Heavy Metals in Rice (Oryzasativa L.) from a Typical E-Waste Recycling Area in Southeast China and Its Potential Risk to Human Health." *Chemosphere* 71.7 (Apr. 2008): 1269–1275. *ResearchGate*. Web. 3 Feb. 2017.

9. Michelle L. Corrigan. "Flame Retardants: A Guide to Current State Regulations." *Lexology*. Globe Business Media Group, 14 June 2016. Web. 3 Feb. 2017.

10. Jack Caravanos, et al. "Assessing Worker and Environmental Chemical Exposure Risks at an E-Waste Recycling and Disposal Site in Accra, Ghana." *Blacksmith Institute Journal of Health & Pollution* 1.1 (Feb. 2011): 16–25. *ResearchGate*. Web. 3 Feb. 2017.

CHAPTER 6. HEALTH EFFECTS OF INFORMAL RECYCLING

1. Xijin Xu, et al. "Chromium Exposure among Children from an Electronic Waste Recycling Town of China." *Environmental Science and Pollution Research* 22.3 (Nov. 2013): 1778–1785. *ResearchGate*. Web. 3 Feb. 2017.

2. Xia Huo, et al. "Elevated Blood Lead Levels of Children in Guiyu, an Electronic Waste Recycling Town in China." *Environmental Health Perspectives* 115.7 (2007): 1113–1117. *ResearchGate*. Web. 3 Feb. 2017.

3. Ibid.

4. Qiaoyun Yang, et al. "Exposure to Typical Persistent Organic Pollutants from an Electronic Waste Recycling Site in Northern China." *Chemosphere* 91. 2 (Jan. 2013): 205–211. *ResearchGate*. Web. 3 Feb. 2017.

5. Li, Yan, et al. "Monitoring of Lead Load and Its Effect on Neonatal Behavioral Neurological Assessment Scores in Guiyu, an Electronic Waste Recycling Town in China." *Journal of Environmental Monitoring* 10.10 (Oct. 2008): 1233–1238. *ResearchGate*. Web. 3 Feb. 2017.

6. Xijin Xu, et al. "Birth Outcomes Related to Informal E-Waste Recycling in Guiyu, China." *Reproductive Toxicology* 33.1 (2012): 94–98. *ResearchGate*. Web. 3 Feb. 2017.

7. "Facts about Stillbirth." *US Centers for Disease Control and Prevention*. US Department of Health and Human Services, 6 Jun. 2016. Web. 3 Feb. 2017.

CHAPTER 7. RECYCLING POLICIES

1. Michael Standaert. "China's Notorious E-Waste Village Disappears Almost Overnight." *Bloomberg BNA*. Bureau of National Affairs, 17 Dec. 2015. Web. 3 Feb. 2017.

2. Ibid.

3. "Government Moves to Tackle E-Waste Pollution." *China.org*. China.org, 25 July 2016. Web. 3 Feb. 2017.

4. "International Agreements on Transboundary Shipments of Hazardous Waste." *EPA*. US Environmental Protection Agency, 7 Dec. 2016. Web. 3 Feb. 2017.

5. Lin Wei and Yangsheng Liu. "Present Status of E-Waste Disposal and Recycling in China." *Procedia Environmental Sciences* 16 (2012): 506–514. *Science Direct*. Web. 3 Feb. 2017.

6. "Parties to the Basel Convention on the Control of Transboundary Movements of Hazardous Wastes and their Disposal." *Basel Convention*. Basel Convention, 2011. Web. 3 Feb. 2017.

7. K. Lines, et al. "Clean and Inclusive? Recycling E-Waste in China and India." *IIED*. IIED, 2016. Web. 3 Feb. 2017.

8. "How U.S. Laws Do (and Don't) Support E-Recycling and Reuse." *Knowledge@Wharton*. Wharton School of the University of Pennsylvania, 6 Apr. 2016. Web. 3 Feb. 2017.

9. "Map of States with Legislation." *Electronics Recycling Coordination Clearinghouse*. Electronics Recycling Coordination Clearinghouse, n.d. Web. 3 Feb. 2017.

10. "How U.S. Laws Do (and Don't) Support E-Recycling and Reuse." *Knowledge@Wharton*. Wharton School of the University of Pennsylvania, 6 Apr. 2016. Web. 3 Feb. 2017.

11. "Update on California's Covered Electronic Waste Recycling Program Implementation of the Electronic Waste Recycling Act of 2003 (SB 20, Sher)." *CalRecycle*. California Department of Recourses Recycling and Recovery, Dec. 2016. Web. 3 Feb. 2017.

12. Chris Van Rossem, Naoko Tojo, and Thomas Lindhqvist. "Extended Producer Responsibility: An Examination of Its Impact on Innovation and Greening Products." *Greenpeace International*. Greenpeace, 27 Sept. 2006. Web. 3 Feb. 2017.

13. "Electronics EPR: A Case Study of State Programs in the U.S." *OCED*. Product Stewardship Institute, 3 June 2014. Web. 3 Feb. 2017.

14. "Michigan Computer Company Owner Sentenced for International Environmental, Counterfeiting Crimes." *US Department of Justice*. US Department of Justice, 22 Mar. 2013. Web. 3 Feb. 2017.

15. "Summary of Criminal Prosecutions, Fiscal Year: 2013." *EPA*. US Environmental Protection Agency, 3 Feb. 2017. Web. 3 Feb. 2017.

16. Krista Torralva. "Texas Law Contributes to Electronics Recycling Boom." *Texas Campaign for the Environment*. Texas Campaign for the Environment Fund, 18 July 2013. Web. 3 Feb. 2017.

17. "Electronics EPR: A Case Study of State Programs in the U.S." *OCED*. Product Stewardship Institute, 3 June 2014. Web. 3 Feb. 2017.

CHAPTER 8. E-WASTE RECYCLING TECHNOLOGY

1. Jennifer Namias. "The Future of Electronic Waste Recycling in the United States: Obstacles and Domestic Solutions." Diss. Columbia University, 2013. *Columbia Engineering*. Web. 3 Feb. 2017.

2. S. Murphy. "Inside Liam, Apple's Super-Secret, 29-Armed Robot that Tears Down Your iPhone." *Mashable*. Mashable, 21 Mar. 2016. Web. 3 Feb. 2016.

3. C. Mars, C. Nafe, and J. Linnell. "The Electronics Recycling Landscape Report." National Center for Electronics Recycling, May 2016. *sustainabilityconsortium.org*. Web. 3 Feb. 2017.

INDEX

ABOUT THE AUTHOR

David M. Barker was born and raised in Canada. He lived for many years in Austin, Texas, where he obtained his doctorate in zoology at the University of Texas at Austin. Dr. Barker has taught and developed educational products in the sciences in the United States and Canada. He now lives in Ontario, Canada, and works as a freelance writer and editor.